INVISIBLE WOMEN OF THE BIBLE

WHAT THEIR STORIES TEACH US — AND WHY
YOUR STORY STILL MATTERS

JENNIFER CARTER

Copyright © 2025 by Jennifer Carter

Published by Hope Books Ltd

All Rights Reserved. No part of this publication may be reproduced in any form or by any means, including scanning, photocopying or otherwise without prior written permission of the copyright holder.

This book is written in British English, so spelling and phrasing may differ slightly from American usage.

Scriptures taken from the Holy Bible, New International Version®, NIV®. Copyright © 1973, 1978, 1984 by Biblica, Inc.™ Used by permission of Zondervan. All rights reserved worldwide. www.zondervan.com

Scripture quotations marked (The Message) are taken from The Message, copyright © 1993, 2002, 2018 by Eugene H. Peterson. Used by permission of NavPress. All rights reserved. Represented by Tyndale House Publishers.

Scripture quotations marked (NLT) are taken from the Holy Bible, New Living Translation, copyright © 1996, 2004, 2007 by Tyndale House Foundation. Used by permission of Tyndale House Publishers, Inc., Carol Stream, Illinois 60188. All rights reserved.

Scripture quotations marked (ESV) are from The Holy Bible, English Standard Version® (ESV®), copyright © 2001 by Crossway, a publishing ministry of Good News Publishers. Used by permission. All rights reserved.

Scripture quotations marked (TPT) are from The Passion Translation®. Copyright © 2017, 2018, 2020 by Passion & Fire Ministries, Inc. Used by permission. All rights reserved. ThePassionTranslation.com.

She gave this name to the LORD who spoke to her: "You are the God who sees me." (Genesis 16:13)

CONTENTS

Introduction : The Bible Women You Were Never Told About   ix
How to Read This Devotional   xiii

PART 1
WHEN THE ROAD AHEAD FEELS UNCERTAIN

1. When Life Doesn't Go As Planned   3
2. The Courage of Commitment   5
3. Divine Appointments   7
4. When No-one Notices : But God Does   9
5. A Love That Changes Everything   11
6. Walking Together Through Suffering   13
7. When You Think Your Best Years Are Behind You   15

PART 2
YOUR STORY ISN'T OVER

8. When Life Isn't Your Choice   19
9. The God Who Sees Me   21
10. Hope in the Waiting   23
11. When Rejection Hits Hard   25
12. When All You Have Are Tears   27
13. Growing in the Wilderness   29
14. Your Story Isn't Over   31

PART 3
WHEN YOU WONDER IF GOD IS STILL THERE

15. When All You Can Do Is Carry On   35
16. When Everything Runs Dry   37
17. The Courage to Say Yes   39
18. When You Have Nothing Left to Give   41
19. When God Provides Just Enough   43

20. When Fear Overwhelms — 45
21. When You Wonder If God Is Still There — 47

PART 4
WHEN YOUR PRAYERS SEEM TO GO UNANSWERED

22. When Heaven Seems Silent — 51
23. Raw and Real with God — 53
24. Strength in the Waiting — 55
25. The Power of Surrender — 57
26. Love That Continues In A New Season — 59
27. The Least Likely Heroine — 61
28. From Grief to Glory — 63

PART 5
WHEN FAITH MEETS DISAPPOINTMENT

29. More Than Just a Busy Woman — 67
30. Lord, Don't You Care? — 69
31. Pulled Away by Distractions — 71
32. Invited to More — 73
33. When You Carry It All Alone — 75
34. Faith in the Midst of Grief — 77
35. He Weeps With You — 79

PART 6
YOU HAVE A PLACE IN GOD'S STORY

36. When God Says Yes (and That's Enough) — 83
37. When God Has Already Spoken — 85
38. The Courage to Follow God's Timing — 87
39. God Uses Ordinary Women in Extraordinary Ways — 89
40. It's Never Too Late to Step Into God's Promise — 91
41. When You Feel Like You Don't Belong — 93
42. You Have a Place In God's Story — 95

PART 7
WHEN IT'S TIME FOR A NEW CHAPTER

43. The Power of Unseen Moments — 99
44. Courage To Do What's Right — 101
45. The Power of Humility — 103

46. Speaking Truth with Wisdom	105
47. The Courage to Be Corrected	107
48. Let God Handle It!	109
49. When It's Time for a New Chapter	111

PART 8
WHEN THE WORLD SAYS YOU'RE DONE—
BUT GOD SAYS THERE'S MORE

50. The Strength of Quiet Defiance	115
51. Small Acts with Great Impact	117
52. When Trusting God Takes Courage	119
53. When Faith Requires Bold Action	121
54. What Happens When You Let Go ...	123
55. When Your Quiet Love Matters	125
56. When Love Becomes Your Legacy	127
Conclusion - The God Who Still Sees	131
One More Thing	133
An Invitation	135
About The Author	139
Sample Chapter from Women of Courage	141
Sample Chapter from Learning to Live in Challenging Times	145

INTRODUCTION : THE BIBLE WOMEN YOU WERE NEVER TOLD ABOUT

Have you ever felt invisible or overlooked, as if *your* story doesn't really matter?

If so, you're not alone.

There are 93 named women in the Bible. Ninety-three. (Plus many more who remain unnamed.) Yet most churches only talk about a handful of them. Martha. Mary. Esther. Ruth. Eve. Maybe Sarah.

But what about Deborah, who led a nation? What about Abigail, whose quick thinking saved her household? Jael, who drove a tent peg through an enemy's head? Or Jochebed, who released her son into an uncertain future and trusted God with what came next?

Their stories are right there in your Bible — but how often do we hear about them? They're incredibly powerful and relevant to us today. And they have so much to teach us.

Women's stories matter. Your story matters. You matter.

Because here's the truth: Jesus saw women. He empowered them, encouraged them, called them to be disciples and witnesses to His resurrection. Paul recognised women like Phoebe as leaders, not afterthoughts.

Our stories need to be told through a lens that understands a woman's heart.

Yet, too often, women's stories have been told by people who've never held a screaming toddler at two in the morning, while wondering how she's going to get the washing done, the home cleaned, and still hold down her job.

But it's not just the daily chaos we carry. It's the deeper things too—the ones we don't always talk about.

Throughout Scripture, we meet women just like us—women who've juggled the impossible, faced heartbreak, walked through overwhelming pain—and kept on walking.

They faced the same fears, doubts, and obstacles that we face. And they asked the same questions: Does God see me? Do I matter? What is God's purpose in all of this?

That's exactly why these "invisible women" speak so powerfully to us today. Their stories remind us: we're not the first to wrestle, grieve, doubt—or long to hope again.

And more importantly, they reveal a God who sees us, knows us, and weaves our stories—even the hardest parts—into His bigger story.

In this book, we'll meet women whose stories have been overlooked for too long. We'll explore their doubts, their courage, their perseverance.

And in their stories, we'll find encouragement for our own journeys. Because the women in these pages are proof: our most powerful moments often come when we say yes to God—and

INTRODUCTION : THE BIBLE WOMEN YOU WERE NEVER TOLD A...

watch Him turn a simple seed of faith into something extraordinary.

These women weren't perfect. They weren't always confident.

But they were seen by God—and so are you.

God isn't done with you. Your story isn't over yet.

HOW TO READ THIS DEVOTIONAL

This book invites you to slow down and spend time with each Invisible Woman of the Bible.

For each woman, there are seven daily readings that dig deeper into her story.

Don't feel you have to rush through these pages.

Make a cup of tea. Find a quiet corner. Take your time.

When something resonates, pause. Read it again. Let it settle into your heart before moving on.

Talk to God about what stirs you or speaks to you.

He met these women. He wants to meet you too.

PART 1

WHEN THE ROAD AHEAD FEELS UNCERTAIN

ONE
WHEN LIFE DOESN'T GO AS PLANNED

"In the days when the judges ruled, there was a famine in the land. So a man from Bethlehem in Judah, together with his wife and two sons, went to live for a while in the country of Moab ... Now Elimelek, Naomi's husband, died, and she was left with her two sons... Mahlon and Kilion, who also died, and Naomi was left without her two sons and her husband." (Ruth 1:1, 3, 5)

Have you ever looked around and thought, "This isn't how I thought my life would go"? Maybe you're standing at a crossroads with no clear way forward? Maybe you're living with loss and pain, unsure of how to move on?

That's exactly where Naomi found herself at the beginning of the book of Ruth.

You might not have heard much about Naomi before—her story often gets overshadowed by Ruth's. But Naomi's story matters.

She and her husband had left Bethlehem because of a famine, hoping for a better life in Moab. But instead of finding stability, Naomi experienced devastating loss.

Her husband died, and then, tragically, both of her sons. She was left alone, a widow in a foreign land, with no-one to provide for or protect her. In that culture, a widow without sons had nothing. No income. No protection. No future.

Sometimes life throws us curveballs we never expected.

Maybe your life doesn't look like you hoped it would. Perhaps you're rebuilding after a divorce, you're widowed, or adjusting to an empty nest in a home that feels far too quiet. Perhaps you're questioning your purpose or wondering where you fit in now.

When life takes an unexpected turn, it's easy to feel unseen, unloved, and forgotten by God.

Naomi felt so bitter and broken that she changed her own name. "Don't call me Naomi—it means pleasant. Call me Mara—bitter—because the Almighty has made my life very bitter" (Ruth 1:20).

But even when Naomi couldn't see it, God was still at work. He hadn't left her. He hadn't forgotten her.

He was about to take her emptiness and give her new purpose and meaning.

Her story wasn't over. And yours isn't either.

Reflection:

Even when you feel empty or like you've lost your purpose, God hasn't stopped writing your story.

Prayer:

Lord, when life doesn't make sense and I can't see You at work, help me remember that my story isn't over. Help me trust that You have more ahead for me. Amen.

TWO
THE COURAGE OF COMMITMENT

"'Look,' said Naomi, 'your sister-in-law is going back to her people and her gods. Go back with her.'"

But Ruth replied, "Don't urge me to leave you or to turn back from you. Where you go I will go, and where you stay I will stay. Your people will be my people and your God my God. Where you die I will die, and there I will be buried. May the Lord deal with me, be it ever so severely, if even death separates you and me." (Ruth 1:15-17)

Have you ever stood at the edge of an unknown future, unsure of what lay ahead?

When Naomi decided to return to Bethlehem, she urged her daughters-in-law, Ruth and Orpah, to stay in Moab. She wanted them to have a chance at a new life, even if it meant saying goodbye.

As they wept together, Orpah kissed Naomi farewell, but Ruth clung tightly to her mother-in-law, vowing: *"Where you go I will go … Your people will be my people and your God, my God."*

Ruth was prepared to give up everything that was familiar to her—her family, her chance to remarry, her country—to step into the unknown with Naomi.

Her words tell us something more, something we could easily miss. When Ruth said, *"Your God, my God"*, she was saying that she had put her trust in the God of Israel. Even after the deep loss she'd suffered, even when the path ahead was unclear, she chose to believe that He would provide and make a way.

As Ruth took that courageous step, she had no idea that God was about to write her story in a way she could never have imagined.

Sometimes God calls us to step into the unknown too. Especially in seasons of change—after the kids leave home, after the loss of a loved one, or when we're entering a new stage of life that feels unfamiliar.

Perhaps He's asking you to step into a new season—of ministry or life. Maybe you need to choose faith when the future looks uncertain. Perhaps you need to let go or move on from someone or something that's close to your heart.

These moments require courage—the courage to say, "I don't know what's ahead, but I know Who goes with me."

Ruth couldn't see what lay ahead. But she knew Who she was following. And that was enough.

Reflection:

Faith sometimes means having the courage to follow where He leads—because you trust the One leading you.

Prayer:

Father, give me the courage to follow You even when the path ahead seems uncertain. Amen.

THREE
DIVINE APPOINTMENTS

"So Ruth the Moabite said to Naomi, 'Let me go to the fields and pick up the leftover grain behind anyone in whose eyes I find favour.' Naomi said to her, 'Go ahead, my daughter.' So she went out, entered a field and began to glean behind the harvesters. As it turned out, she was working in a field belonging to Boaz, who was from the clan of Elimelek." (Ruth 2:2-3)

Have you ever looked back on a "coincidence"—only to realise that God had been guiding you all along?

After they arrived in Bethlehem, with no husband to provide for them, Ruth went out to glean—gathering leftover grain from the harvest. She ended up in the field of Boaz, a wealthy relative of Naomi's.

Boaz heard about Ruth and how she'd cared for her mother-in-law, and he saw past the dust-covered clothes—to the character of the woman beneath. He chose to go far beyond what the law required, to provide for and protect this stranger.

Ruth didn't choose Boaz's field—she just went out to glean, and "happened" to land in the field of a kinsman-redeemer, a close relative who had the power to step in and change everything for her and Naomi.

But was it really just chance? Or was God guiding her steps, even when she couldn't see it, weaving together the threads of her story?

What looked like a random choice was actually a divine appointment. And I believe that's true for us too.

Think back over your own life. When have you experienced what seemed like a random moment that later revealed itself as so much more? Maybe it was a door that opened when you least expected it. A call from a friend just when you needed encouragement. A move to a new church where you ended up meeting people who changed your life.

What looks random to you has never been random to God. Those moments—the ones we dismiss as luck or coincidence—may actually be God's carefully orchestrated providence.

Even now, that unexpected conversation, that nudge you can't explain, that door that's starting to open—it might be God directing your steps from behind the scenes.

Ruth didn't see God's hand that day. But it was there. It's there in your story too.

Reflection:

What feels like coincidence may be God guiding your every step.

Prayer:

Lord, help me trust that You are weaving together the threads of my story into something beautiful. Amen.

FOUR
WHEN NO-ONE NOTICES : BUT GOD DOES

"Boaz replied, 'I've been told all about what you have done for your mother-in-law since the death of your husband—how you left your father and mother and your homeland and came to live with a people you did not know before. May the Lord repay you for what you have done. May you be richly rewarded by the Lord, the God of Israel, under whose wings you have come to take refuge.'" (Ruth 2:11-12)

Have you ever kept praying, kept waiting—and heard nothing but silence?

Ruth was someone Boaz could easily have overlooked. She may have felt invisible as she quietly gathered leftover grain.

But listen to what Boaz said: "I've been told all about what you have done."

Her faithfulness, her loyalty, her hard work—none of it had gone unnoticed. Boaz's words reveal a deep truth: she had been seen all along.

Day after day, Ruth was doing the most mundane work possible, just to survive. As a foreign woman working alone in the fields, she faced real dangers—harassment, exploitation, even violence. Yet she went anyway, trusting God to protect her. And He did.

God saw every risk she took, every act of quiet courage.

Sometimes in our seasons of waiting, when it feels like nothing is happening or changing, we wonder if anyone sees our struggles or our small acts of faithfulness. We wonder if it really matters.

Just because you feel lost doesn't mean God has lost sight of you. In those moments when it feels as if you're drifting, God may actually be doing some of His most important work.

God doesn't waste a single moment of our journey. He is always at work, even when we can't see it.

That unexpected encouragement that lifted you this week. The provision that came just when you needed it. The peace that settled over you when nothing had actually changed—these are God's fingerprints on your life, His way of saying, "I see you. I'm working on your behalf. Trust me."

Just as Ruth was seen in her season of waiting, so are you.

God sees your faithfulness, even when no-one else is watching. He sees your integrity, when it would be easier to cut corners. He sees every kindness, every prayer, every sacrifice.

None of it is wasted. None of it goes unseen.

Reflection:

You may feel as if no-one sees your quiet faithfulness, but God does.

Prayer:

Father, thank You that, even when I feel invisible, You see me. Amen.

FIVE
A LOVE THAT CHANGES EVERYTHING

"Then Boaz announced to the elders and all the people, 'Today you are witnesses that I have bought from Naomi all the property of Elimelek, Kilion and Mahlon. I have also acquired Ruth the Moabite, Mahlon's widow, as my wife ..." (Ruth 4:9-10)

Have you ever looked at your life—the mess, the ordinary bits, the disappointments—and wondered if God could really use any of it?

Ruth had been reduced to picking up grain from the ground to feed herself. Yet Boaz married her and redeemed the land that had belonged to Naomi's family.

The wealthy landowner married a penniless foreign widow. It's a surprising reversal that reminds us that even when our story feels messy, God can take the broken pieces and weave them into something beautiful. That's just who He is.

But here's what we often miss—Ruth wasn't the only one being redeemed. Before he met her, Boaz was wealthy but alone—no children, no legacy, no future beyond his wealth.

Ruth gave Boaz what his money could never buy—a family and a son. The redeemer was himself redeemed.

And Ruth, the outsider, became the great-grandmother of King David and a part of Jesus' lineage. Her faithfulness didn't just change her life—it changed the lives of Naomi, Boaz, and all the generations who would come after them.

She simply did what she could, faithfully and with love. No grand gestures. Just quiet obedience, day after day. And God used that.

And the same is true for you and me. He can use our daily choices, our small acts of obedience, of love and kindness, to redeem the world around us.

We often think of God's work as something He does *for* us—and it is! But amazingly, He can also work *through* us to touch the lives of others.

Maybe you feel like your life is too ordinary to matter. Or too messy. Or too broken.

But Ruth's story shows us—you don't need to have all the answers. You don't need to wait until you have a perfect life. You just need to keep showing up.

God took Ruth's messy story and wove it into His story. He can do the same with yours.

Reflection:

Your story isn't too messy for God to use. Just keep showing up and being faithful in the small things.

Prayer:

Father, help me trust that You can use my life—even the messy bits—to bring hope to others. Amen.

SIX
WALKING TOGETHER THROUGH SUFFERING

At this they wept aloud again. Then Orpah kissed her mother-in-law goodbye, but Ruth clung to her." (Ruth 1:14)

Have you ever had the kind of friend who was there for you, no matter what?

The story of Ruth and Naomi is a story of the power of true friendship.

Their bond broke barriers of age, nationality, and circumstance. They cried together, lived together, and held one another when times were tough.

In a world that can feel so fragmented, their story is a reminder of how much we need one another—and challenges us to build deeper, more committed friendships—the kind that don't walk out when life gets messy.

It takes real love to be the kind of friend who walks alongside others when their lives are breaking and their hearts are hurting.

But isn't that exactly what Ruth did for Naomi? She didn't just offer words of comfort—she walked alongside her, she stood beside her in her pain, she shared in her sorrow and refused to let her go alone.

It was an act of love that required sacrifice—a willingness to simply be present. And isn't that exactly what Jesus does for us?

True redemption isn't just about rescuing someone—it's about walking with them, standing beside them in the pain, and refusing to let them go alone.

Jesus meets us in our deepest sorrow and refuses to leave us there. He steps into our pain, walks with us through it. And this changes everything.

Sometimes the most powerful thing we can do isn't to fix someone's problems—it's to refuse to let them face those problems alone.

We all need people who will walk with us through our darkest valleys. And we all have the opportunity to be that person for someone else.

Sometimes the greatest gift someone can give us isn't answers, but simply being there.

Reflection:

Jesus already gave us the gift of never having to face our darkest valley alone. He is walking with you.

Prayer:

Jesus, thank You for being the friend who never leaves. Help me to know Your presence in my darkest valleys. Amen.

SEVEN
WHEN YOU THINK YOUR BEST YEARS ARE BEHIND YOU

"The women said to Naomi: 'Praise be to the Lord, who this day has not left you without a guardian-redeemer. May he become famous throughout Israel! He will renew your life and sustain you in your old age. For your daughter-in-law, who loves you and who is better to you than seven sons, has given him birth.'

Then Naomi took the child in her arms and cared for him. The women living there said, 'Naomi has a son!' And they named him Obed. He was the father of Jesse, the father of David." (Ruth 4:14-17)

Do you sometimes feel as if the best parts of your life are over?

So did Ruth, Naomi, and Boaz.

Ruth was a foreigner. Penniless. She was starting over with nothing. Simply gleaning leftover grain, just trying to survive.

Naomi was a bitter and broken woman who had invested everything in her family, only to watch it all fall apart. She thought her life was over.

Boaz was a wealthy man who had everything—except a wife and family to share it with.

It looked as if their story was over. Yet their greatest chapter was still to come.

Each of them surrendered what little they had to God. Ruth surrendered her homeland. Naomi surrendered her bitterness. Boaz surrendered his comfort.

God was already at work, and He took those broken pieces and wove them into something beautiful. Even in their darkest moments, He was working behind the scenes, writing their story into His story.

Naomi held her grandson and found new purpose. Ruth became a wife and mother. Boaz became a father at last. And that baby—Obed—became the grandfather of King David and part of the lineage of Jesus Himself.

God used three broken people to change history. And He can do the same with you.

So if you've ever felt "too broken," "too old," or "too insignificant"—remember that your story isn't over. God's not done with you yet.

Reflection:

Even in your most ordinary moments, God is at work, preparing something better than you might imagine.

Prayer:

Father, when I feel overwhelmed by today's demands or uncertain about tomorrow's purpose, help me trust that You're still writing my story. Amen.

PART 2
YOUR STORY ISN'T OVER

EIGHT
WHEN LIFE ISN'T YOUR CHOICE

"Now Sarah, Abram's wife, had borne him no children. But she had an Egyptian slave named Hagar; so she said to Abram, 'The Lord has kept me from having children. Go, sleep with my slave; perhaps I can build a family through her.'" (Genesis 16:1-2)

Have you ever felt swept along by circumstances you didn't choose? Or as if you're living a story that someone else wrote?

That's where we find Hagar. A slave woman without status, voice, or choice.

Hagar's story begins with someone else's decision. She doesn't ask to be part of the plan. She isn't invited into the conversation. She is used to fulfil Sarah's longing for a child.

It's hard to read. And it may be hard to relate to the cultural context of the story—but what's not hard to understand is the feeling of being swept up in something you didn't choose.

Maybe you've been there. Perhaps you know that feeling.

Maybe you've been trapped in circumstances beyond your control—a difficult marriage, a health diagnosis, or a situation where someone else was calling all the shots.

Perhaps it was a marriage that didn't last, a job loss that turned your life upside down or a family that drifted apart. Maybe it's just the quiet ache of being left to pick up the pieces.

Like Hagar, you might feel like you're living in a story that someone else wrote.

And yet—God steps in.

He doesn't avoid the mess. He enters it.

He doesn't wait for us to sort ourselves out first. He meets us right where we are.

Hagar may have been invisible to Sarah and Abraham—but she was not invisible to God. Even before she ran, He saw. Even before she cried, He knew.

And He would meet her in the desert and speak to her directly—something that very few in Scripture experience so intimately.

You may feel like your life has spun beyond your control. But it has never spun beyond God's care. He sees what you didn't choose. He hears what others ignored. And He is with you in it.

Reflection:

Even when you feel powerless or caught up in someone else's story, that's the very place where God meets you.

Prayer:

Lord, there are parts of my story that I never would have chosen. Situations I couldn't control. But You are the God who sees, who steps in and meets me in the middle of the mess. Amen.

NINE
THE GOD WHO SEES ME

"She gave this name to the Lord who spoke to her: 'You are the God who sees me,' for she said, 'I have now seen the One who sees me.'" (Genesis 16:13)

Have you ever felt invisible? Maybe you've poured yourself out for others, held it together through your heartache—and it felt like no-one noticed.

Hagar didn't choose this life—she was Sarah's slave given to Abraham to bear a child on her behalf, then cast aside, an object of scorn.

When Hagar fell pregnant, something shifted. Perhaps there was a hint of pride in her eyes—she had achieved the one thing Sarah desperately wanted. Whether real or imagined, Sarah felt her contempt. And jealousy turned to cruelty.

She mistreated Hagar so badly that she ran. Alone. Afraid. Pregnant. With no destination—just away. Away from pain. Away from rejection. Away from everything. And into the desert.

That's exactly where God met her.

The angel of the Lord appeared to her near a spring. This is the first time in Scripture the angel of the Lord appears—and not to a king or a prophet, but to a pregnant, runaway slave. She is not even one of His chosen people.

And there, in the desert, the angel spoke to her. Not with condemnation, but with compassion.

He called her by name, "Hagar, servant of Sarah." And asked gently: "Where have you come from, and where are you going?"

That moment wasn't about fixing everything overnight. It was about being seen. Known. Called by name.

Because Hagar wasn't invisible to God. Not for a moment.

And in that moment, she gave God a name: El Roi—*the God who sees me*. Because being seen—truly seen—meant everything.

And maybe that's what your heart needs today, too. To know that even when no-one else seems to notice, God does.

When your prayers feel quiet and your tears feel wasted, He sees you. He knows your name, your past, and your heart. And He is not absent from your story.

Reflection:

Even when the world overlooks you, God sees you.

Prayer:

El Roi, the God who sees me—thank You that when no-one else seems to notice, You do. Help me hold onto that truth today. Amen.

TEN
HOPE IN THE WAITING

"Abram was eighty-six years old when Hagar bore him Ishmael." (Genesis 16:16)

Have you ever grown tired of waiting on God?

God had made Abraham an extraordinary promise—that his descendants would be as numerous as the stars in the sky. But Sarah was barren. She had lived with heartbreak for years.

And year after year, nothing changed.

Ten years is a long time to wait.

It's not hard to understand, is it? The ache of a deferred dream. The month-after-month heartbreak. The spiritual confusion of knowing God said something—and then not seeing any sign that it's actually happening.

We can judge Sarah for taking matters into her own hands, but can't we also relate?

You pray, you hope, you wait—and after a while, your faith starts to fray at the edges. You wonder if maybe you misheard God, or worse, that He's gone quiet.

Sometimes waiting wears us down until we start looking for a shortcut. A compromise. A plan B that might not be what God intended, but at least it feels like *something*.

And in her desperation, Sarah suggests a solution to Abraham—that Hagar, her slave, should bear him a child.

But her solution only created more pain. And isn't that the way it often goes when we try to manufacture fulfilment on our own?

It would have been so much better to wait for God's timing. Of course, that's easier said than done—especially when what we're hoping for seems impossible.

But God hadn't abandoned His promise. He didn't disqualify Sarah for her impatience. He met her in the mess and kept His word anyway.

God's timing is not always our timing. His delays are never dismissals.

That door that hasn't opened? That prayer that feels unanswered? That dream still on hold? God's silence isn't rejection.

"Not yet" isn't "no."

Reflection:

Even in the waiting, God is still at work—writing a story you can't yet see.

Prayer:

Lord, when the waiting feels long and my hope runs thin, help me not to rush ahead, but to rest and trust in Your promises. Amen.

ELEVEN
WHEN REJECTION HITS HARD

"Then Sarah said to Abraham, 'Get rid of that slave woman and her son, for that woman's son will never share in the inheritance with my son Isaac.'" (Genesis 21:10)

Rejection has a way of lodging itself deep in the heart, doesn't it?

It's one thing to feel overlooked. It's another thing entirely to be told outright: *You don't belong. You're not welcome. You're not wanted.*

That's exactly what happened to Hagar.

After years of living in Abraham's household, after bearing his child, after raising her son under the same roof—she was cast out.

Not gently. Not with compassion. But with a cruel command: "Get rid of that slave woman and her son."

There's no kindness in those words, no recognition of the years she served, or the pain she might feel.

To Sarah, she was simply a problem to be solved. And to Abraham? He was deeply distressed, but ultimately, he let her go.

Hagar and her son were sent into the wilderness, away from her home and her community. Discarded like she never mattered.

But that rejection? What looked like abandonment was actually redirection—God was leading her down a path she would never have chosen to take.

The most painful thing—Sarah's jealousy and rejection—became the very thing that set Hagar free.

What Sarah meant for evil, God used for good (Genesis 50:20).

Hagar walked into that wilderness a slave. She walked out of it a free woman.

And her son Ishmael—the boy Sarah wanted gone—became the father of nations.

But here's the thing: Hagar couldn't see that in the moment. It was only as she looked back that she could see God had been in it all along.

And one day, you'll see it too. Maybe this side of heaven. Maybe the other side. But one day, it will all make sense.

Reflection:

You may not be able to see past the hurt right now—and that's okay. But one day, when you look back, you'll see His fingerprints on every chapter—even this one.

Prayer:

Father, I don't understand every chapter of my story. Help me trust that one day I'll look back and see Your hand in all of it. Amen.

TWELVE
WHEN ALL YOU HAVE ARE TEARS

"God heard the boy crying, and the angel of God called to Hagar from heaven and said to her, 'What is the matter, Hagar? Do not be afraid; God has heard the boy crying as he lies there.'" (Genesis 21:17)

Have you ever been so caught up in your pain that you can't see the way forward?

That's where Hagar finds herself in Genesis 21.

The water has run dry. Her son is crying. She sits under a bush and weeps because she cannot bear to watch him die.

This woman who has already endured so much has reached her lowest point.

There's no record of her crying out to God. She didn't utter a formal prayer. But God sees Hagar in her distress—and His heart goes out to her.

The angel calls to Hagar: "Do not be afraid. God has heard the boy crying." And then, so tenderly, He opens her eyes. There, in front of her, is a well.

Hagar gives her son a drink. They will live.

Provision she hadn't seen. Hope she didn't know was there. A future she thought was lost. Not a lightning bolt miracle—but just what she needed for that day.

God heard Ishmael crying. He heard Hagar weeping. He heard the cry of her heart—even when she had no words for it.

Sometimes our prayers never make it into words. Sometimes, prayer sounds like sobbing your heart out when there are no words to say.

There are seasons when we don't know what to pray—when the dreams we built have shattered, when the hurt runs too deep, when starting over seems impossible.

We don't need eloquent words when we pray. Sometimes the cry of our heart or our tears are prayer enough.

Because God knows our hearts. He knows our deepest desires and our greatest fears.

So if all you have today are tears, know this: God hears them.

And He is near.

Reflection:

Even when words fail, your tears are enough—because God hears the cry of your heart.

Prayer:

Lord, thank You that You hear my heart even when I can't find words. When I'm overwhelmed, help me remember You are near and open my eyes to Your provision. Amen.

THIRTEEN
GROWING IN THE WILDERNESS

"God was with the boy as he grew up. He lived in the desert and became an archer." (Genesis 21:20)

Have you ever found yourself in a hard place and wondered, "What did I do wrong to deserve this?"

Hagar found herself in the desert twice. The first time, she ran. The second time, she was driven out.

But God wasn't any less faithful the second time around. He didn't say, "You should have learned this lesson already." He met her with the same compassion, the same provision, the same presence.

Let's not rush past what Hagar had just experienced. She had wept. She had feared for her son's life. She had reached the end of herself.

And yet, God showed up. He spoke to her. He opened her eyes. He pointed her to provision.

This is who our God is—He is the God who sees, the God who provides, and the God who stays present, even when others walk away.

And here, we see the outcome of that encounter: Ishmael grows. He becomes strong. He makes a life. He learns to thrive in the very wilderness that once nearly ended his story.

The desert wasn't a punishment. It wasn't a sign that Hagar had missed God's plan. It was the place where God met her, provided for her, and grew her son into a man.

Sometimes we worry that the wilderness will break us—or break our children. But Hagar's story reminds us that God can cause growth anywhere, even in the middle of a desert.

We want comfort, stability, and a clear path forward. And yet, sometimes, the desert is where God teaches us the most. It's where He deepens our roots. It's where we learn resilience. It's where we learn to rely on Him in ways we never would in abundance.

Hagar may not have had the life she would've chosen. But the last thing we read in her story isn't despair—it's hope.

If you're looking at your life and wondering whether anything good can come from your wilderness, remember this: God is still writing your story. And He is with you *in even here.*

Reflection:

The desert that threatens to break you may be the very place where God grows you strongest.

Prayer:

Lord, thank You that You don't just rescue me—you stay with me. Even in places I'd never choose for myself. Amen.

FOURTEEN
YOUR STORY ISN'T OVER

"Then God opened her eyes and she saw a well of water." (Genesis 21:19)

Have you ever felt defined by your past? By what's happened to you? By the labels others have put on you?

Hagar's story has been one of powerlessness from the beginning. And there, in the desert, it must have felt as if her story was over.

At nearly every turn, other people made decisions about her life. She was a slave, a surrogate, cast out when jealousy flared.

She only did what she was told to do. She didn't ask for any of this. And yet she found herself in the wilderness, not once, but twice.

If anyone had the right to be defined by her brokenness, to be bitter or to allow resentment to take root, it was Hagar.

But that's not how God saw her. And it's not how her story ends.

There's something quietly extraordinary about Hagar's ending—not with fireworks, but with survival, strength, and steady hope.

She was seen. She was rescued. And she was given the strength to carry on.

Sometimes, we need to hear that God's provision doesn't always look like we expect it to. Sometimes it looks like a well in the wilderness.

The child who was left to die in the wilderness didn't just survive—he thrived. He became the father of a great nation. That's legacy.

And Hagar? She rebuilds. No longer a victim of other people's decisions—she's writing her own story now.

Your story may have chapters that feel messy, broken, unjust, or unfinished. You may look back and think, "I never would have chosen this path."

But your brokenness doesn't define you. Your backstory doesn't define you. What's happened to you doesn't define you.

God sees you differently. And He's not finished with you yet.

When you're tempted to think your story is over—He whispers, *It's not.*

Reflection:

What looks like an ending might just be where God begins something new. Your story isn't over yet.

Prayer:

Lord, help me believe that what's happened to me in my life doesn't define who I am to You. Thank You that You're still writing my story—and You're not finished yet. Amen.

PART 3
WHEN YOU WONDER IF GOD IS STILL THERE

FIFTEEN
WHEN ALL YOU CAN DO IS CARRY ON

"Then the Lord said to Elijah, 'Go and live in the village of Zarephath, near the city of Sidon. I have instructed a widow there to feed you.' So he went to Zarephath. As he arrived at the gates of the village, he saw a widow gathering sticks ..." (1 Kings 17:8-10 NLT)

Have you ever felt like you were down to nothing?

Maybe it wasn't literally your last bit of food, but perhaps you've reached the end of your emotional strength, your financial resources, your patience—or your hope.

In these verses we meet a woman gathering sticks.

She was a widow—one of the poorest and most vulnerable in that society—and there was a famine in the land. She was preparing what she believed would be the last meal for herself and her son before they starved to death.

Elijah asked her for a drink and a piece of bread, and her response was heartbreaking, "I don't have any bread—only a handful of flour in a jar and a little olive oil in a jug. I am gathering a few sticks to take home and make a meal for myself and my son, that we may eat it—and die."

The mention of her gathering sticks is a simple detail, but it speaks volumes.

She was at her lowest point, facing starvation, but she was still doing the one thing she could for herself and her son. Even when the flour was almost gone, she had the courage to keep gathering sticks.

There was something beautiful about her quiet courage. She didn't rage or despair. She did the next small thing.

And isn't that what faith is sometimes? Just showing up. Doing what you can. Trusting God with the rest?

She could have given up. She could have stayed home and wept. She could have raged against God or complained about her circumstances. She didn't do any of those things.

She got up. She gathered sticks. She did the one small thing she could. And because she was out there—doing what she could—she was in the right place at the right time.

Faith isn't just waiting for God to show up—it's doing your bit, and trusting God to meet you in it.

Keep gathering sticks.

Reflection:

When you're tempted to give up hope, remember that even your smallest step of faith is an invitation for God to meet you there.

Prayer:

Lord, give me the quiet courage to keep going—even when I can't see the way forward. Amen.

SIXTEEN
WHEN EVERYTHING RUNS DRY

But after a while the brook dried up, for there was no rainfall anywhere in the land. (1 Kings 17:7 NLT)

Have you ever had something dry up in your life—a role, a job, a relationship, a season—and wondered, "What now?"

Before Elijah met the widow, God had been providing for him by a brook. Birds brought him bread and meat every morning and evening, and he drank from the brook.

But then comes this quiet little verse: "Some time later the brook dried up."

These words reveal something profound about how God works. Even though God had been providing, and Elijah had done everything right, the brook still dried up.

Maybe you've experienced that—a comfortable situation, maybe even a good one, and then suddenly, it's gone. The kids move out, your season changes, a door closes—and you're left feeling confused, maybe even a little abandoned.

And here's what stings: you did everything right. Just like Elijah. And still, the brook dried up.

It doesn't seem fair, does it? When you've been faithful and things still fall apart. When you've done your best and the ground shifts beneath you anyway.

But sometimes, when that happens, it's not punishment. It's not failure. It's God seeing the bigger picture—and moving us on. Not cruelly, but with purpose.

Here's what I love about this story. While Elijah was sitting by that dried-up brook, the widow was already running out of flour.

Two people, both at the end of their resources—and God was about to move them toward each other. At the exact moment the widow was gathering sticks for her last meal, help was already on its way.

Neither of them could see it. But God could.

When we read this story, we often see ourselves as the widow—waiting for our answer to arrive. But maybe you're Elijah—being moved on from something comfortable toward something you can't yet see.

Either way, the truth is the same: God knows exactly what He's doing. You just need to trust Him.

Reflection:

When God moves you on, you may not know why—but it's always with purpose.

Prayer:

Lord, when things run dry, help me trust that You're already at work—even if I can't see it yet. Amen.

SEVENTEEN
THE COURAGE TO SAY YES

"She went away and did as Elijah had told her." (1 Kings 17:15)

Have you ever sensed God prompting you to do something—and talked yourself out of it?

This story shows us two people, both trusting God—and God working through both.

First, there's Elijah. How did he know which widow God had chosen? There was no angel pointing the way, no divine sign hovering over her home—just God's command to go.

So Elijah did what we see others do throughout Scripture: he made a simple request and watched for God to show him the answer.

Elijah arrived at the town gate, saw a woman gathering sticks, and made a simple request: "Would you bring me some water and a piece of bread?"

He trusted God to show him. And God did.

When God told Elijah, "I have instructed a widow there to feed you," it sounds like she was expecting him, doesn't it? But she had no idea what was coming! So what did God mean?

I believe He had prepared her heart. Something in her spirit recognised this was from God—even if her head couldn't explain it.

Hebrews 11:8 says that Abraham went, not knowing where he was going: "By faith, when called to go to a place he would later receive as his inheritance, he obeyed and went, even though he did not know where he was going."

Elijah went, not knowing how the widow would meet him. The widow said yes, not knowing what would happen.

Both trusted. Both obeyed *before* they understood. And God met them in it.

That's what real faith looks like. Not waiting until you have all the answers. Not needing to understand "why," before you move.

Faith is doing what He asks—even when it doesn't make sense yet. Especially when it doesn't make sense yet.

Reflection:

Faith isn't about always understanding why—it's about doing what He asks, and trusting Him with the rest.

Prayer:

Lord, give me the courage to obey before I understand. Help me trust Your promptings—and act on them. Amen.

EIGHTEEN
WHEN YOU HAVE NOTHING LEFT TO GIVE

"Elijah said to her, 'Don't be afraid. Go home and do as you have said. But first make a small loaf of bread for me from what you have and bring it to me, and then make something for yourself and your son.'" (1 Kings 17:13)

But first. Those two words are easy to miss. But they change everything.

Elijah doesn't say, "Feed yourself and your son, and if there's anything left over, bring me some." He says, "But first, make a small loaf for me."

He's asking her to give before she meets her own need. To share her last meal with a stranger—before she knows how the story ends.

But Elijah's request comes with a promise: 'For this is what the LORD, the God of Israel, says: The jar of flour will not be used up and the jug of oil will not run dry until the day the LORD sends rain on the land.' (1 Kings 17:14)

She had a choice. Trust the promise—or hold onto what little she had.

That's the thing about God's promises—they give us the courage to do what we couldn't do on our own.

She didn't give blindly. She gave because she had a word from God.

And we have promises too. Promises that He will provide. Promises that He will never leave us. Promises that He is faithful.

In Malachi 3:10, God says: 'Test me in this... and see if I will not throw open the floodgates of heaven and pour out so much blessing that there will not be room enough to store it.'

The question is: do we trust Him enough to act on His promise.

The world's economy says, "Make sure you've got enough before you give." But God's economy says, "Give—so that you will have all that you need." It's the opposite of everything we're taught.

Here's what the world will never understand: stop waiting until you have enough to give. Give—and then you'll have enough.

God's economy says give first. Trust Him with the rest.

That's what the widow of Zarephath did. She gave her last meal. And it opened the door to God's supernatural provision.

Reflection:

When God invites you to test Him, it's because He's that confident in His faithfulness.

Prayer:

Lord, I choose to trust Your promises today. Help me hold what I have with open hands. Amen.

NINETEEN
WHEN GOD PROVIDES JUST ENOUGH

"For the jar of flour was not used up and the jug of oil did not run dry, in keeping with the word of the LORD spoken by Elijah." (1 Kings 17:16)

What if God's provision in your life isn't meant to look like having it all, but rather *just enough* for today? What if the miracle isn't that He removes the hardship, but that He sustains you through it, one day at a time?

The widow does exactly what Elijah told her to. She makes bread for him first—giving away what should have been her last meal—and then discovers the miracle: "The jar of flour was not spent, neither did the jug of oil become empty."

God provided enough flour and oil each day. Not an abundance, not enough to store up—just enough for what they needed each day.

But His provision isn't just about food, is it? We run out of so much more than that. Wisdom. Patience. Courage. Hope. It's so easy to come to an end of ourselves.

And sometimes God's provision doesn't mean changing our circumstances—it means strengthening us in the middle of them. He provides what we need each day, and He walks with us through it.

Here's the invitation for us—to trust God for today's provision rather than worrying about tomorrow's needs. And, just as God did for this widow, He promises to provide what we need—even if it's just what we need for today.

Perhaps you've been praying for God to dramatically change your circumstances—to heal the illness completely, to instantly restore the relationship, to immediately resolve the financial difficulty.

Yet, sometimes His provision looks more like strength for today, wisdom for the next conversation, or peace when the future feels uncertain.

When Jesus taught us to pray for our "daily bread," He was inviting us into a daily dependence, saying, "Don't worry about having everything figured out."

That's the kind of God we have. He may not always give us what we need in advance, but He gives us what we need, when we need it.

Just enough for today *is* enough.

Reflection:

God's provision isn't always abundance—sometimes it's just enough for today. And that is enough.

Prayer:

Father, when I start worrying about what's ahead, remind me that You've got today covered, and You'll have tomorrow covered too. Amen.

TWENTY
WHEN FEAR OVERWHELMS

"Some time later the woman's son became sick. He grew worse and worse, and finally he died." (1 Kings 17:17 NLT)

Have you ever carried a fear you don't speak out loud? Been faithful on the outside and lived with a silent dread?

The story takes an unexpected turn. Here's this woman who was doing everything right. God had been miraculously providing for her. And yet, her son dies. It just doesn't make sense.

Her response to Elijah is revealing: "What do you have against me, man of God? Did you come to remind me of my sin and kill my son?"

Her words reveal a belief many of us carry—that suffering is punishment for something we've done.

This widow had been carrying a secret fear all along—that despite all God had done for her, her past sins would eventually catch up with her. That she deserved to suffer because of her past mistakes.

Have you ever wondered why so much suffering came upon Job? There *is* an answer held within the pages of your Bible.

In Job 3:25, Job says, "What I feared has come upon me; what I dreaded has happened to me."

It wasn't Job's sin that caused his suffering—it was his fears.

But here's the truth: if you're in Christ, Jesus already dealt with every past mistake on the cross.

And yet so many of us live as if that's not true. We carry a quiet dread that one day we'll get what we deserve.

That quiet dread? It's fear.

There's a reason that the Bible tells us, "Do not fear," over and over again. Because fear and faith cannot live in the same space, any more than light and dark can exist together.

To know true freedom, we need to let go of fears—to name them, and bring them into the light.

What fear might you be carrying today—one you've never spoken out loud?

You don't have to carry it anymore.

Name it. Bring it to God. And let it go.

Reflection:

God is saying to you today: "Do not fear."

Prayer:

Father, thank You that I don't have to carry my fears anymore. Help me trust You with all of them. Amen.

TWENTY-ONE
WHEN YOU WONDER IF GOD IS STILL THERE

"Then the LORD heard Elijah's cry, and the boy's life returned to him, and he lived... Then the woman said to Elijah, 'Now I know that you are a man of God and that the word of the LORD from your mouth is the truth.'" (1 Kings 17:22–24)

Can you remember the last time you knew—really knew—that God was there?

Sometimes God allows us to reach the very end of ourselves—not just our physical resources, but our emotional and spiritual ones too—before He reveals His power.

What happens next is extraordinary. Elijah takes the boy's body to his upper room, stretches himself out on the child three times, and cries out to the Lord. God hears his prayer—the boy's life returns to him.

When Elijah brings the child back, the widow makes a profound declaration: "Now I know that you are a man of God and that the word of the LORD from your mouth is the truth."

Her real miracle wasn't the flour or the oil. It was when she could finally say those words: "Now I know."

There's a difference between believing God can provide and knowing He will. She'd seen daily provision for months—and still carried fear. It took this moment for her to move from believing to knowing.

Those are the mountaintop moments we need to hold onto. The times when God showed up. When we knew—really knew—that He was real and He was faithful.

Maybe you've had moments like that. Maybe you've seen God come through in ways you couldn't explain.

Because there will be days when the fear creeps back, when doubt whispers, when we wonder if God is still there.

And it's in those valleys that we need to remember our mountaintop moments—the moments we knew God showed up.

The Israelites set up stones of remembrance—so they wouldn't forget what God had done (Joshua 4:6-7). We need to do the same.

Remember them. Write them down.

Your mountaintop moments are your stones. Hold onto them.

Reflection:

Hold on to your mountaintop moments and remember God's faithfulness when you're in the valley.

Prayer:

Father, thank You for the times You've shown up. Help me remember each one. Amen.

PART 4
WHEN YOUR PRAYERS SEEM TO GO UNANSWERED

TWENTY-TWO
WHEN HEAVEN SEEMS SILENT

"In bitterness of soul Hannah wept much and prayed to the LORD. And she made a vow, saying, 'LORD Almighty, if you will only look on your servant's misery and remember me, and not forget your servant but give her a son, then I will give him to the LORD for all the days of his life.'" (1 Samuel 1:10-11)

Have you ever prayed for something so deeply that your heart ached?

That's exactly where Hannah found herself. Year after year, her prayers for a child seemed to fall on deaf ears. And the Bible tells us something that makes it even harder to understand: the Lord had closed her womb.

How do you make sense of that? It wasn't just disappointment. She must have sometimes wondered if God Himself was holding back from her, perhaps even punishing her.

To make matters worse, her husband's other wife, Peninnah, seemed to participate in God's blessing so easily—child after child, again and again—while Hannah had nothing.

Peninnah didn't let her forget it, provoking her and making her life miserable.

Hannah lived in a culture where a woman's worth was measured by her ability to bear children. Each time she went to Shiloh with her family to worship, her pain was magnified—surrounded by other families with their children, a constant reminder of what she lacked.

Hannah knew that God had promised fruitfulness, yet that very fruitfulness was denied to her. How could she reconcile God's promises with her own painful reality?

Perhaps you know what that's like—to long for something deeply, something that others around you seem to receive easily? Maybe it's not a child, but a relationship, an opportunity, or a dream that feels out of reach?

It can be challenging to watch others receive answers to their prayers while heaven seems silent for you. But Hannah's story teaches us something powerful: unanswered prayers don't mean unheard prayers. God heard every single one.

Hannah couldn't see the bigger story God was writing through her waiting—every prayer stored up in heaven, every one heard all along.

Reflection:

Your unanswered prayers aren't unheard. He's heard every single prayer—and He's still at work, writing your story.

Prayer:

Lord, when heaven seems silent, help me remember that You hear every cry of my heart. Help me trust that You're preparing something I can't yet see. Amen.

TWENTY-THREE
RAW AND REAL WITH GOD

"Hannah was praying in her heart, and her lips were moving but her voice was not heard. Eli thought she was drunk and said to her, 'How long are you going to stay drunk? Put away your wine.' 'Not so, my lord,' Hannah replied, 'I am a woman who is deeply troubled. I have not been drinking wine or beer; I was pouring out my soul to the LORD.'" (1 Samuel 1:13-15)

Have you ever been in so much pain that you couldn't even find the words to pray? Perhaps tears came instead, or maybe just raw sounds of pain that you couldn't control. Our most authentic prayers often come when we're at our breaking point.

That's exactly where Hannah found herself. Every year, Elkanah would take his family to Shiloh to worship. As they went up to Shiloh, everything was geared around family.

If you've ever been in a church where everything centres on families, perhaps even felt that you just don't fit in, you know something of Hannah's experience.

It was during one of these trips that Hannah's pain reached breaking point. Hannah didn't hide her pain from God or put on a brave face and pretend everything was fine. She brought every raw emotion to Him.

Her grief was so raw, her prayer so intense, that Eli the priest thought she'd been drinking. But Hannah wasn't ashamed to explain that she was pouring out her soul before the Lord.

Even in her brokenheartedness, God was the One Hannah turned to. Sometimes we think our painful emotions are too ugly for Him to handle, but Hannah poured every single one of her raw feelings out to God.

Have you ever reached that point—where your prayers move beyond polite requests to raw, pain-filled cries?

So often we approach God with our 'Sunday best prayers'—polite, proper, and perfectly composed. But Hannah's story reminds us that God wants our authentic hearts more than our polished words.

At your lowest point, when the pain feels unbearable, He is still a safe place—a place to unburden yourself, to be honest, to be raw and real.

He can handle it all.

Reflection:

You don't have to have the right words. Just bring your heart—messy emotions, unfulfilled longings and deep disappointments.

Prayer:

Lord, thank You that I can come to You just as I am—no masks, no pretending, no holding back. Help me be real with You in every season. Amen.

TWENTY-FOUR
STRENGTH IN THE WAITING

"Year after year this man went up from his town to worship and sacrifice to the LORD Almighty at Shiloh... Whenever the day came for Elkanah to sacrifice, he would give portions of the meat to his wife Peninnah and to all her sons and daughters. But to Hannah he gave a double portion because he loved her, and the LORD had closed her womb." (1 Samuel 1:3, 4-5)

Have you ever dragged yourself to church when everything in you wanted to stay home and cry?

Hannah was faithful in her waiting. Year after year, she kept going up to Shiloh. She continued worshipping, continued praying, continued bringing her pain to God—even when nothing seemed to change.

Patience is perhaps one of the hardest spiritual disciplines. In our instant-everything world, the concept of waiting years—even decades—for a prayer to be answered feels almost unbearable.

But the waiting isn't wasted time. He's forming in you the wisdom and heart you'll need for the next chapter He is writing.

Hannah went to the temple—the one place she believed she could find God. Despite her pain. Despite her heartbreak. She still sought Him.

Year after year, she kept coming back—still seeking, still asking, still hoping He would show up and intervene. She refused to give up on God, even when it seemed He had given up on her.

There was no sign that anything would ever change. And yet she kept taking the pain to God. She stayed faithful. She brought her brokenness to God.

And her faithfulness went even deeper. In her prayer, Hannah made a vow: 'Lord, if you give me a son, I will give him back to you for all the days of his life.'

Most of us pray with our hands open to receive. Hannah prayed with her hands open to give. That's so powerful.

Being a Christ-follower isn't about having it all together. It's about trusting God and believing He is for you, even when all the evidence tells you otherwise.

Maybe you're in that place right now—still seeking, still waiting, still hoping.

Keep showing up. Keep bringing it all to Him. Keep trusting.

That's real faith.

Reflection:

Faith is showing up—bringing your pain to God—even when nothing seems to change.

Prayer:

Lord, give me the strength to keep showing up. Help me worship while I wait, trusting that You are working even when I cannot see it. Amen.

TWENTY-FIVE
THE POWER OF SURRENDER

"After he was weaned, she took the boy with her, young as he was... and brought him to the house of the LORD at Shiloh... She said, 'Pardon me, my lord. As surely as you live, I am the woman who stood here beside you praying to the LORD. I prayed for this child, and the LORD has granted me what I asked of him. So now I give him to the LORD. For his whole life he will be given over to the LORD.'" (1 Samuel 1:24-28)

Have you ever received something you deeply longed for, only to sense God asking you to surrender it back to Him?

After years of waiting, God answered Hannah's prayer. She conceived and gave birth to a son, Samuel.

Suddenly everything in her life changed. She had a child to pour out her love on. There was no more reproach. She could finally hold her head up.

The most remarkable part of Hannah's story is what comes next. Hannah kept her vow.

When he was still a young child, she took him to the house of the Lord in Shiloh and presented him to Eli the priest.

Her words to the priest take my breath away: "I prayed for this child, and the Lord has granted me what I asked of him. So now I give him to the Lord."

The child she had prayed for, wept for, and finally received—she handed over to be raised by someone else in service to God. That's surrender.

Years of waiting had taught her to trust God's purposes over her own. And Hannah didn't forget who gave her this gift. She kept her word to the One who kept His.

Everything in her must have wanted to hold on to her son. Fear would have told her that surrendering her only child would leave her with nothing. But Hannah trusted God more than she feared the emptiness.

And He didn't leave her empty. God gave her three more sons and two daughters.

She gave one. God gave her five.

Surrender didn't leave her empty. Because, when you surrender what you love most to God, it's held by the One who loves you most.

Reflection:

When God asks you to let go, it's not so that you end up empty. Oftentimes, it's so that He can fill your hands with more.

Prayer:

Lord, help me hold Your blessings with open hands. Give me the courage to surrender back to You whatever You ask. Amen.

TWENTY-SIX
LOVE THAT CONTINUES IN A NEW SEASON

"Each year his mother made him a little robe and took it to him when she went up with her husband to offer the annual sacrifice." (1 Samuel 2:19)

Have you ever handmade something for somebody special?

When we create something with our own hands for someone we love, every stitch, every moment becomes an act of devotion. Our thoughts turn to them repeatedly as we work, and our love is literally woven into the fabric.

There's a beautiful detail tucked into Hannah's story—each year, she would make Samuel a little robe and bring it to him at Shiloh. This small act speaks volumes about her heart.

We can only imagine Hannah making those garments—taking the wool, carding it, spinning it, weaving it. At every step, she poured her love into this child she could no longer care for daily.

What makes Hannah's story even more remarkable is that she trusted her son to Eli when his own sons were so out of control.

Yet it seems that God put a hedge of protection around Samuel. Perhaps Hannah's faithful prayers made all the difference.

Even though she had surrendered her son to God's service, Hannah's love didn't stop. She simply found a new way to show it. Surrender didn't mean she stopped being his mother—it meant being his mother in a different way.

Perhaps you've had to surrender something precious too—maybe a relationship that changed, a child who moved far away, a dream that needed to be laid down, or a ministry that came to an end.

Maybe you've found yourself in a season where the old ways of loving and caring for a loved one are no longer possible—whether through distance, changed circumstances, or life transitions that require you to step back.

Hannah's story teaches us that surrender doesn't mean the end of love. It means finding new ways to express that love within God's calling.

Like Hannah's robe, your prayers wrap around those you love. Even when you can no longer hold them close—whether through distance or estrangement—you can still hold them up to God. Your prayers reach when your arms cannot.

Reflection:

Your prayers wrap around those you love—no distance is too far.

Prayer:

Lord, thank You that my prayers still reach those I love. Help me trust that when I hold them up to You, You hold them safe. Amen.

TWENTY-SEVEN
THE LEAST LIKELY HEROINE

"He raises the poor from the dust and lifts the needy from the ash heap; he seats them with princes and has them inherit a throne of honour." (1 Samuel 2:8)

Have you ever looked around and thought, "Why would God use me?" Perhaps you've reached a stage of life where you feel overlooked or undervalued. Maybe your children have grown and moved away, or a relationship has ended, leaving you wondering about your purpose.

If you had walked through Hannah's village and asked, "Who is God most likely to reveal Himself to? Who might become great among these people?" Hannah would have been the least likely candidate. You probably wouldn't even have noticed her.

Peninnah seemed strong, thought she had power. She had children and status.

Eli's sons had privilege, position, and power. They took for themselves the best of the sacrifices, yet they neither knew nor respected the God their father served.

Yet, it was Hannah, the one everyone overlooked, that God used to change history.

Not Peninnah. Not Eli's privileged sons. Hannah.

This reveals an important truth: having even the wisest of parents doesn't guarantee spiritual awareness or wisdom. Each of us must find our own way to God. No one can walk that path for us.

And often it's those of us who have struggled, wrestled with disappointment, but who have nevertheless surrendered to God and trusted Him, who truly understand something of the heart of God.

Hannah was one of those. This seemingly insignificant woman set in motion events that would change the course of history.

Her son Samuel became the nation's spiritual leader, anointing King David—from whose line Jesus would be born. And it was Jesus who told us that many who are first shall be last, and the last will be first.

That was certainly true for Hannah. And it can be true for you.

Hannah's story reminds us that everything is not what it seems from the outside. Your strength isn't measured by what the world sees, but by the quiet trust you place in the God who sees it all.

Reflection:

Your significance is not determined by society's measure of success, but by your faithfulness to the One who sees what others cannot.

Prayer:

Lord, thank You that You don't measure worth the way the world does. Help me to be faithful in the quiet moments. Amen.

TWENTY-EIGHT
FROM GRIEF TO GLORY

"Then Hannah prayed and said: 'My heart rejoices in the LORD; in the LORD my horn is lifted high... The LORD brings death and makes alive; he brings down to the grave and raises up. The LORD sends poverty and wealth; he humbles and he exalts.'" (1 Samuel 2:1, 6-7)

Have you ever noticed how God has a way of bringing something good out of our painful journeys? The very places that once brought us the most heartache often become the sources of our greatest joy and testimony.

That's what happened for Hannah. The annual trip to Shiloh once filled her with dread and grief. It meant enduring Peninnah's taunts and confronting her own emptiness once again.

But now, the journey to Shiloh was different. She held her head up high, filled with excitement and anticipation.

Hannah's story shows that God is the One who can turn even seemingly impossible things around, who delights in turning mourning into dancing.

Listen to Hannah's own words: *"He raises the poor from the dust and lifts the needy from the ash heap; he seats them with princes and has them inherit a throne of honour."* (1 Samuel 2:8)

She wasn't just reciting what she knew *about* God. She was telling her story. She had lived it.

Her breakthrough came through trusting God, being raw and honest with Him, and surrendering to Him.

That day in the temple when she poured her heart out to God, when Eli thought she was drunk, must have seemed like the end of the world, but God hadn't finished with her story yet.

This is often God's pattern.

The wilderness seasons, the times of waiting and weeping, eventually give way to seasons of abundance and joy. Not always in the ways we expect, but in ways that reveal His greater purpose and faithfulness.

Whatever grief or disappointment you're experiencing today, know that it doesn't have the final word. God wants to meet you right in the middle of the mess and carry you through.

He can take your endings and turn them into beginnings. He can take your deepest pain and turn it into your greatest purpose.

Reflection:

God wastes nothing—not your tears, not your waiting, not your pain. It all has purpose.

Prayer:

Father, I trust You with the chapters I can't yet see. Thank You that You're not finished writing my story yet. Amen.

PART 5
WHEN FAITH MEETS DISAPPOINTMENT

TWENTY-NINE
MORE THAN JUST A BUSY WOMAN

"'Martha, Martha,' the Lord answered" (Luke 10:41–42)

Can I be honest? I've always felt Martha gets a bit of a bad rap.

We're told that while her sister Mary sat at Jesus' feet, Martha was busy getting everything ready. And Jesus corrected her?

It seems a little unfair, doesn't it?

Think about it—David committed adultery, Sarah doubted, Abraham lied, Eve disobeyed… but Martha's 'mistake'? She was too hospitable?

Now, of course there's more to the story than that, but let's keep things in perspective. Martha was doing her best to serve Jesus.

She wasn't doing anything wrong—she was doing something good, even expected! In that culture, hospitality was a big deal. Honouring your guests meant everything.

So why did Jesus correct her?

Let's look at what He said: "Martha, Martha." He uses her name twice. That's significant. We see it elsewhere in Scripture at powerful, pivotal moments—"Abraham, Abraham." "Moses, Moses." "Samuel, Samuel." When God repeats your name, something important is happening. It's almost like Jesus is saying, *Lean in, this really matters.*

Then He says, "You are worried and upset about many things, but few things are needed—or indeed only one." It wasn't her serving that was the issue. It was that her heart had become pulled away—distracted.

She was trying to serve Jesus without actually spending time with Him. And gently, lovingly, He called her back. And honestly? I think a lot of us know that feeling.

Life is full of many things—good things, necessary things. But when we get caught up in the doing, when we carry all the weight and pressure to get it right, we can easily miss the invitation to just be with Him.

Jesus wasn't comparing Martha to Mary in order to shame her. He saw that Martha needed reminding that she was *already* loved—and didn't need to earn it by running herself ragged.

That same reminder is for us today: you are loved before you lift a finger.

Reflection:

You were loved before you lifted a finger. You still are.

Prayer:

Jesus, when I get pulled in too many directions, remind me that You already love me. Help me choose time with You over striving. Amen.

THIRTY
LORD, DON'T YOU CARE?

"Martha was distracted with much serving. She came to Him and said, 'Lord, don't you care that my sister has left me to serve alone? Tell her to help me!'" (Luke 10:40)

Have you ever had one of those days where everything just gets on top of you and you finally snap?

It's rarely about what's happening in the moment. Often, it's all those little things we've quietly carried, day after day—until finally, the load feels too heavy to bear.

I know, I've had moments like that. And, to me, this feels like one of *those* moments for Martha.

She's in her own home, hosting Jesus and His disciples—unexpected guests, at that. And she's doing her best to offer proper hospitality, which was a huge cultural expectation.

She's preparing the food, serving everyone, making sure it all runs smoothly. And all the while, Mary is sitting at Jesus' feet, not lifting a finger to help.

And so Martha says what many of us have probably felt: "Lord, don't you care?"

There's such honesty in those four words.

Maybe it wasn't just about Mary not helping. Maybe Martha felt alone in the work, unappreciated, and unseen.

And her frustration bursts out, not in a calculated complaint, but in a raw, weary cry from an anxious heart.

I love that Jesus doesn't shame her for it.

He doesn't shut her down or send her away. He hears the cry beneath her words—the cry of a weary woman who feels unseen—and answers with love.

And, He gently redirects her focus and calls her back to what matters most. Not the cultural expectations. Not the busyness. Not even the long to-do list. *Just Him.*

For every woman who has ever felt taken for granted, left to shoulder the load, or invisible in her serving—this moment reminds us that Jesus sees what others overlook, and He cares for the one who feels unseen.

So, maybe today, if you're feeling like Martha—overloaded, overlooked, or left carrying the weight on your own—hear Him gently calling you back too.

Reflection:

When the weight feels too heavy and the question rises, 'Lord, don't You care?'—His answer is always, 'You don't have to carry this by yourself.'

Prayer:

Lord, I feel like I'm holding everything together and no-one sees. But You do. Help me turn to You today. Amen.

THIRTY-ONE
PULLED AWAY BY DISTRACTIONS

"'Martha, Martha,' the Lord answered, "'you are worried and upset about many things.'" (Luke 10:41)

Jesus' words to Martha could just as easily be spoken over us today: 'You are worried and upset about many things.'

Isn't that so true for many of us? Our hearts so easily get weighed down by many things.

Sometimes, we don't even realise how many things we're carrying. Yesterday's struggles, today's responsibilities, tomorrow's worries—they swirl together inside our minds, a whirl of emotions, decisions, and distractions.

What I find comforting is that Jesus doesn't say, "You're doing too much."

He says, "You are *worried and upset*." He sees beyond the doing to the heart behind it. The inner life. The emotional load you've been carrying in silence. The weariness no-one else sees. The worries that sit heavy on your heart.

The Passion Translation says Martha was *"pulled away by all these many distractions."* Isn't that what it feels like sometimes?

Pulled in a hundred directions—not by bad things, but by ordinary responsibilities, roles we've carried for years, people who depend on us. These are often good things, necessary things, even meaningful things.

But when they pile up and press in from every side, they can leave us feeling weary, scattered, and stretched thin. And the truth is—even good things can distract us from the best thing: simply being with Jesus.

The Message expresses Jesus's words like this: *"You're fussing far too much and getting yourself worked up over nothing."*

At first, that can sound a little confronting. But I think He said it with a smile and with love. Because so often, when we look back on those moments, what we got worked up over seems like nothing.

Martha was distracted, pulled away, worried, and upset. Not because she didn't care—but maybe because she cared too much.

And Jesus saw her. And instead of more demands, He offered her something better—His presence. His peace.

Reflection:

Sometimes it isn't that we care too little, but that we care so much we forget to simply rest with the One who cares most.

Prayer:

Jesus, You see my heart. You know the distractions and the worries that weigh me down. I don't want to be pulled away—I want to be drawn in. Help me to lay down what I can't control and simply sit with You today. Amen.

THIRTY-TWO
INVITED TO MORE

"Mary has discovered the one thing most important by choosing to sit at My feet. She is undistracted, and I won't take this privilege from her." (Luke 10:42 TPT)

This story in Luke takes place in Martha's home, and we need to remember how deeply important hospitality was in that culture.

Hosting guests was expected. It was honourable. She was doing what generations of women before her had taught her to do—putting everyone else's needs first, ensuring everything was perfect, carrying the weight of responsibility on her shoulders.

And while we often picture Martha as having a stressful day, there may have been more going on. Because what Mary was doing—sitting at Jesus' feet—wasn't just unusual, it was bold. That posture was reserved for disciples, and women didn't belong there.

In a world where women were expected to stay in the background, serve quietly, and not presume to learn alongside the men, Mary was breaking every social rule.

Perhaps Martha's frustration wasn't only that Mary had left her to serve alone. Maybe she was embarrassed. Maybe even angry. After all, she was the one left to keep everything running on her own.

How must that have felt? Was she tired of always being the one in the background?

How many of us have felt this way? We've spent years being the dependable ones, the ones who make sure everything gets done, who sacrifice our own needs for others. And then someone else gets recognised for stepping outside those expectations while we're still in the kitchen, left carrying the load.

But what's beautiful is how Jesus responds. He sees both Martha *and* Mary. He doesn't dismiss Martha's service—instead, He gently redirects her attention to what matters most, inviting her to reorder her priorities.

He's saying, "Martha, your heart to serve is beautiful, but don't let it distract you from the greater gift I'm offering—My presence. I love you as you are, not for what you do."

And His invitation was never for Martha alone. It's for us. Because it's never too late to say yes.

Wherever you are today—Jesus is still saying, "Choose what is better. Choose time with Me."

Reflection:

Jesus sees past your roles and invites you into His presence—not for what you do, but simply because you are loved.

Prayer:

Lord, thank you that You see me and invite me into the same closeness You offered to Mary. Help me not to miss it. Help me take my place at Your feet. Amen.

THIRTY-THREE
WHEN YOU CARRY IT ALL ALONE

"As Jesus and his disciples were on their way, he came to a village where a woman named Martha opened her home to him." (Luke 10:38)

Have you ever felt like everything depends on you? Maybe you've become the one everyone calls when things need sorting. Perhaps you feel that, if you don't hold it all together, no-one else will?

It's not that we mean to live like this. We just sort of slide into it. Especially when we've always been the "capable one." The responsible one. The strong one.

When Jesus said that Martha was worried and upset about many things, He was talking about more than preparing a dinner. He was talking about all the thoughts that filled her mind, the mental load she carried.

He knew that her struggle wasn't the busyness—it was about trusting Him. Could she trust that the world wouldn't fall apart if she stopped for a moment?

Martha was doing what she thought needed to be done. But Jesus invited her to trust Him with what she *couldn't* control.

In a world that often feels out of control, our instinct is to grip tighter—to manage every outcome, anticipate every problem, hold everything together by sheer effort.

We try to fix not only today's problems, but tomorrow's problems as well.

But it's exhausting. And He never asked us to carry it all.

The *many things* that worry us often come from a place of love. We care about people. We want things to go well. And it's hard to let go, to trust the people we love to Him. To leave them in His hands.

But what if we could care deeply without carrying the weight of outcomes? What if we could love well while leaving the results in His hands?

That's the invitation Jesus offered Martha. Not to stop caring, but to care from a place of trust instead of control.

He still does.

His invitation is to let go. To give it all to Him. And to leave it there.

Reflection:

You don't have to hold it all together. Jesus invites you to trust Him with all those things you care about, but can't control.

Prayer:

Jesus, I'm tired of holding it all together. Help me let go—and actually leave it with You. Amen.

THIRTY-FOUR
FAITH IN THE MIDST OF GRIEF

"'Yes, Lord,' she said, 'I believe that You are the Messiah, the Son of God, who is to come into the world.'" (John 11:27)

Martha shows up again in the gospel of John. And this time, she's grieving because her brother Lazarus has died.

In the midst of her loss, she runs out to meet Jesus, saying, "If You had been here, my brother wouldn't have died."

It wasn't an accusation. It was simply her truth.

But she didn't stop there. She then made one of the boldest declarations of faith in the New Testament: "Lord, I believe that You are the Messiah, the Son of God."

What's so powerful is when she said it. Because she said it before the miracle. Before Lazarus was raised. Before she saw anything change.

Her faith wasn't based on the outcome—it was rooted in who Jesus is.

In that moment, when all hope seemed gone, Martha still chose to anchor herself in the unchanging truth of who Jesus is. She clung to the promise of life, even while standing at her brother's tomb.

Her faith was not dependent on circumstances. She trusted in who Jesus was, believed in Him, in the face of deep loss. She believed before the miracle—that is real faith.

That's the kind of faith I want.

And I love that Martha—who's so often seen as just the flustered woman in the kitchen—is also the one who, in her grief, showed incredible faith and proclaimed truth with strength and courage.

Martha's story gives us permission to be human. To have our moments of frustration, our honest cries of "where were You?"—while still maintaining a deep and honest faith.

We can be both. Grieving and believing. Honest about our pain and anchored in who He is.

Maybe you're in a season of waiting right now. The answer hasn't arrived. The situation still looks impossible.

Martha shows us that faith doesn't require seeing first. We can say "I believe" even when, humanly, the situation seems hopeless—even while we're still standing at the tomb.

Reflection:

Faith is about holding on to who He is, even when you don't know what's ahead. You can whisper "I believe" through tears.

Prayer:

Jesus, I want the kind of faith that trusts you before the answer comes. Amen.

THIRTY-FIVE
HE WEEPS WITH YOU

"Jesus wept." (John 11:35)

We often rush past this verse—the shortest in the Bible—without stopping to feel its weight.

Jesus is standing with Martha. Her brother Lazarus is dead. And Jesus—who already knows He's about to raise Lazarus from the grave—weeps.

He doesn't say, "Don't worry, I've got this." He doesn't rush to fix it. He doesn't stand at a distance.

He is moved with compassion. His heart goes out to her. He weeps.

He enters her grief. He feels it with her.

This is who Jesus is.

He doesn't wait for our tears to dry or our circumstances to change before He comes close. He meets us right in the middle of it all.

I think sometimes we expect Jesus to show up with solutions. We want Him to fix it, explain it, or fast-forward us to the other side of the pain. And sometimes He does.

But sometimes, He simply weeps with us first.

That's not weakness. That's love.

Martha had just declared her faith—"I believe You are the Messiah." And how does Jesus respond? Not with a sermon. Not with a rebuke. Not even with the miracle—not yet.

First, He grieves with her.

Maybe you're in a season of heartbreak right now. Loss. Disappointment. A door that's closed. A prayer that feels unanswered.

And maybe you've wondered if Jesus even cares.

He does. More than you know.

He isn't standing at a distance, arms crossed, waiting for you to pull yourself together. He's right there with you. In the mess. In the tears. In the middle of the night when sleep won't come.

Jesus meets us in our deepest sorrow and refuses to leave us there. He weeps with us, steps into our pain, and walks with us through it. And that changes everything.

Reflection:

Jesus doesn't always rush in to fix your pain. Sometimes He sits with you in it first.

Prayer:

Jesus, thank You for entering my grief—not to fix it, but to be with me in it. Amen.

PART 6
YOU HAVE A PLACE IN GOD'S STORY

THIRTY-SIX
WHEN GOD SAYS YES (AND THAT'S ENOUGH)

"Now Deborah, a prophet, the wife of Lappidoth, was leading Israel at that time." (Judges 4:4)

Have you ever felt overlooked, or found yourself waiting for someone to invite you into your calling? If so, this story is for you.

For 20 years the Israelites were cruelly oppressed by Sisera, commander of the Canaanite army. Finally, the people of Israel called out to God for help.

And onto the stage stepped Deborah, who God had called to be one of his judges. Unlike kings, whose role was inherited, each judge was chosen directly by God. They brought spiritual wisdom and provided leadership in times of crisis.

The text doesn't mention any resistance to her leadership because she was a woman. Nobody questioned her authority. She simply took her place as the judge God had appointed.

What is remarkable about Deborah's story is that God seems to have called her directly.

She didn't seek anyone's approval—she simply stepped into what God had called her to. And He does the same with us.

Too often, we as women wait for someone to invite us to lead or speak or take part. But the truth is, that invitation may never come.

Does that mean God hasn't placed a call on your life? Of course not!

And if you're an older Christian woman—don't count yourself out. You've spent decades building wisdom, experience, and spiritual maturity. Why would God set all that aside? What if everything you've walked through isn't a limitation—but the very qualification He's looking for?

God has a plan and a purpose for you—He created you and equipped you uniquely for the work He's calling you to. You don't need to wait for anyone's permission or invitation. It's up to you to step into it.

So listen closely. Consider what He has laid on your heart. Take small steps of faith, and watch what He can do when you're faithful to follow Him wherever He leads.

When God speaks to your heart, you don't need anybody else's approval—you just need His yes.

Reflection:

You don't need anyone's permission to step into God's calling—His yes is enough.

Prayer:

God, thank You that I don't need anyone else's approval to walk in the calling You've placed on my life. Help me be faithful to that small whisper—and to follow wherever You lead. Amen.

THIRTY-SEVEN
WHEN GOD HAS ALREADY SPOKEN

"One day she sent for Barak son of Abinoam ... She said to him, 'This is what the Lord, the God of Israel, commands you: Call out 10,000 warriors from the tribes of Naphtali and Zebulun at Mount Tabor.'" (Judges 4:6 NLT)

Deborah had been judging Israel faithfully, but the people were still living under the cruel oppression of Sisera's army.

God had already spoken to Barak, Israel's military commander, about leading the army into battle, but he had hesitated. So Deborah, stepping into her role as prophetess, sent for him.

When she spoke to him, she reminded him of what God had already said, "Hasn't God already told you to gather the army and go down to face Sisera?"

As a military leader, perhaps he had good reason. The Canaanites, under Sisera, had 900 iron chariots—a formidable force that could move swiftly and effectively against foot soldiers, giving them a huge tactical advantage.

No wonder Barak hesitated—from a human perspective, victory must have seemed impossible.

So Deborah instructed Barak, "Go, gather your men at Mount Tabor, taking 10,000 from the people of Naphtali and the people of Zebulun. And I will draw out Sisera, the general of Jabin's army, to meet you by the river Kishon with his chariots and his troops, and I will give him into your hand."

Barak replied, "I will go, but only if you go with me."

His words echo Ruth's beautiful declaration—"Where you go, I will go"—but without Ruth's courage.

So Deborah answered him, prophesying, "I will go with you. But, the road on which you are going will not lead to your glory, for the LORD will sell Sisera into the hand of a woman."

God had a winning strategy for an Israelite army faced with overwhelming odds. It was not about human strength or weapons, but about calling His people to trust and obey Him.

And it's the same for us today. So often, we want God to map everything out before we take the first step—and so we hesitate. But faith asks us to take the first step, trusting He'll direct the rest.

Reflection:

When God speaks, you don't have to figure everything out. Just take the next step.

Prayer:

Lord, forgive me for the times I've hesitated when You've already spoken. Help me to follow where You lead. Amen.

THIRTY-EIGHT
THE COURAGE TO FOLLOW GOD'S TIMING

"Deborah said to Barak, 'Go! This is the day the LORD has given Sisera into your hands. Has not the LORD gone ahead of you?'" (Judges 4:14)

Deborah, sensing God's timing, urges Barak, "Up! For this is the day in which the LORD has given Sisera into your hand. Does not the LORD go out before you?"

These words are incredibly powerful! She's reminding Barak that even though the situation seems impossible, God is promising victory.

She reminds him that it's the Lord who is truly leading the charge in this battle—that he is simply following behind Him. Her words are deeply encouraging because she is telling him that God is ultimately in control, and that makes all the difference.

For a military man facing seemingly impossible odds, her words would have stirred courage—courage to trust that God would do the impossible.

Just as He had done before, God can use the smaller and weaker army to defeat the stronger one. The victory was already secured in the spiritual realm; Barak simply had to go and take hold of that victory in the natural world.

We see this pattern repeated throughout the pages of our Bibles. We see this pattern throughout Scripture. In Gideon, taking 300 men against 135,000. In David, a shepherd boy defeating the giant Goliath.

Each faced overwhelming odds, but when God leads them and promises victory, they simply need to step into that promise and take hold of it to see it fulfilled.

As the army marched, it rained. The river Kishon became a torrent. Those 900 iron chariots—the very thing they trusted in, the source of their pride and power—got stuck in the mud. God turned what they relied on into their downfall.

So the Lord won the battle. He routed Sisera's army, scattering them into confusion and panic, crushing them completely. Sisera himself fled on foot.

And the same is true for us. When God speaks, He goes before us —if we will only be courageous enough to take the next step.

The victory was already theirs. They just had to show up. And so do you.

Reflection:

When God goes ahead of you, then no matter how lost or powerless you feel, it's time to rise up and act, because the victory is already won.

Prayer:

Father, thank You for going before me into every battle. Help me to sense Your timing and to move when You say "This is the day!" Amen.

THIRTY-NINE
GOD USES ORDINARY WOMEN IN EXTRAORDINARY WAYS

"Jael went out to meet Sisera and said to him, 'Come, my lord, come right in. Don't be afraid.'" (Judges 4:18)

But the story isn't over yet, because this is where Jael enters the picture.

When Sisera arrives, as dictated by the laws of hospitality, Jael goes out of her tent to meet him. Exhausted after the battle, he asks for some water. But Jael gives him milk to drink and then covers him with a rug.

He begs her to deny that he's present if anyone comes looking, then falls fast asleep from exhaustion. And it's here that Jael's role changes from hospitable wife to warrior woman.

Because at some point Jael decided to kill Sisera. We don't know exactly when, perhaps it was before he arrived. Perhaps she had heard of Deborah's prophecy, or perhaps it was only as he lay there sleeping that God revealed his plan to her.

What we do know is that Deborah prophesied that a woman would kill this man, and that Jael was the fulfilment of that prophecy.

While Sisera slept, Jael reached for what was to hand—a tent peg and a hammer. Not a soldier's weapons. Just the ordinary tools of a woman who pitched tents for a living. And God used them to bring down a commander.

She drove the peg through his temple, killing him instantly. Deborah's prophecy was fulfilled: a woman had defeated Israel's enemy.

Jael took a huge risk. If Sisera had woken, there is no doubt that, as an experienced military man and leader, he could have overwhelmed Jael and killed her in a few seconds.

As we reflect on this story, it can seem hard to contemplate that such a violent act was the will and purpose of God.

We see it throughout history—God using ordinary women with ordinary means to change the world. Joan of Arc. Rosa Parks. Corrie ten Boom. Ordinary women. Extraordinary impact.

The question isn't whether you're qualified—it's whether you'll trust that, with God, what's already in your hands is enough.

Reflection:

You don't need special skills or new qualifications. God will use what's already in your hands.

Prayer:

God, thank You that You use ordinary women for Your extraordinary purposes. Help me see that what I already have is enough for what You're calling me to. Amen.

FORTY
IT'S NEVER TOO LATE TO STEP INTO GOD'S PROMISE

"On that day God subdued Jabin king of Canaan before the Israelites." (Judges 4:23)

This story takes place about 150–200 years after Israel first entered the promised land. After Joshua died, the people didn't fully drive out the nations as God had commanded, leading to compromise and idolatry.

Because of that disobedience, they found themselves under the heavy hand of Jabin, King of Canaan, for 20 long years.

What's happening here is really about reclaiming what God had already promised them—land they had once taken, but then lost.

Throughout the Old Testament we see a pattern: God's people fall short, God allows an enemy to rise up against them, they cry out for help, and God rescues them. Again and again, this cycle repeats.

When God first told Israel to go in and take the land, some refused to enter.

Only Joshua and Caleb—who believed God's promise—lived to see it fulfilled.

Now, years later, we see the same lesson playing out again. God had already given them the victory—they just had to step forward and claim it. This time, they did.

Both times God had already won the victory. One generation waited 40 years. The other, a matter of hours.

This cycle—falling short, crying out, being rescued—isn't failure. It's how God keeps drawing us back. Despite his hesitation, Barak is still named in Hebrews 11's Hall of Fame. His wobble didn't disqualify him. And yours won't disqualify you either.

How often do we experience this in our own lives? We can know God's calling on us, but can find ourselves hesitating, fearful or on the back foot. This story reminds us that with God, even after failure, there is always a second chance.

When God makes us a promise, He's inviting us into a divine partnership. He has already given us the victory, but we still have to step forward in faith to claim it.

Is there something that God has promised you, a battle He's promised you'll win, a 'land' He's promised you'll enter?

Will you trust Him enough to take the first step?

Reflection:

Your wobble doesn't disqualify you. God is still inviting you to step into all that He's promised.

Prayer:

Father, thank You that even when I hesitate or hold back, You've never given up on me. Thank You for second chances. Amen.

FORTY-ONE
WHEN YOU FEEL LIKE YOU DON'T BELONG

"Most blessed of women be Jael, the wife of Heber the Kenite, most blessed of tent-dwelling women." (Judges 5:24 & 26)

Have you ever wondered what on earth Jael's husband said when he got home?

Picture it: he walks into his tent expecting supper—and finds the commander of the Canaanite army dead on the floor, a tent peg through his skull, blood everywhere. They were supposed to be *friends* with the Canaanites. We can only imagine that conversation!

Here's what makes Jael's story so remarkable: she wasn't an Israelite. Her family was allied with the Canaanites. She was an outsider.

We don't know how God spoke to her—only that she responded. And God took this neutral woman, this outsider, and used her for His purposes.

And here's the part that takes my breath away: she wasn't just used—she was *celebrated*.

In Deborah and Barak's victory song, Jael is called "most blessed of women." Not tolerated. Not mentioned in passing. Celebrated. Honoured.

An outsider. A woman whose family had made peace with the enemy. And yet God wove her into His story—and then lifted her up.

For God looks at the heart—as He did with David, so He did with Jael—and so He does with us.

So, just because you're different to other Christian women, don't count yourself out. If you've ever felt like you don't quite fit—like you don't have the right background, the right credentials, the right church history—this story is for you.

God doesn't wait for you to belong before He uses you. He meets you where you are—and invites you in.

Jael had none of the qualifications we might expect. And yet God chose her, used her, and celebrated her.

The world draws circles to define who belongs. But God? He just redraws the circle bigger to include you.

Reflection:

You don't have to earn your way into God's story. God already has a place for you.

Prayer:

Lord, thank You for redrawing the circle to include me. Thank you that I belong. Amen.

FORTY-TWO
YOU HAVE A PLACE IN GOD'S STORY

"For all of God's promises have been fulfilled in Christ with a resounding "Yes!" And through Christ, our "Amen" (which means "Yes") ascends to God for his glory." (2 Corinthians 1:20 NLT)

There can hardly be a starker contrast: Deborah, powerful, strong, a leader of the nation. And Jael, a tent-dwelling woman, an outsider to Israel, yet brought into His story at just the right moment.

Both were chosen, both were anointed. Both were right where God needed them to be, at just the right time.

If we learn anything from this story, it's that the women God calls do not fit into a neat mould. God raises up unlikely heroes.

Esther, a queen in a palace. Paul, a former persecutor. Mary, a girl from a nowhere town. Deborah, a prophet. Jael, a homemaker with a tent peg.

All very different. All called by God.

And so are you.

God doesn't just call the anointed—He anoints the called.

It's so tempting to look at other women and see their gifts—to wish we might be more like them. But your calling won't look like theirs. It's not meant to. That's not who God has made you to be—and it's not an accident, it's by design.

So often, we wait until we feel ready. Until the kids are older. Until we have more time. Until someone notices us and asks. But that's not how God works.

You don't need to have it all figured out. He'll equip you as you go.

The Red Sea only parted when the Israelites took the first step. God didn't clear the way and then ask them to walk. He asked them to walk—and then cleared the way.

Deborah didn't wait for permission—she stepped into God's call. So did Jael. And you can too.

So listen to what God has laid on your heart. Take small steps of faith. Be willing when He invites you to partner with Him—and see what He might do.

God doesn't need you to look or act like anyone else. He just needs you to be you.

Reflection:

God doesn't need you to look like anyone else. He just needs you to be you.

Prayer:

Father, I don't have it all figured out. But You do. Help me take the first step—trusting that You'll equip me as I go. Amen.

PART 7

WHEN IT'S TIME FOR A NEW CHAPTER

FORTY-THREE
THE POWER OF UNSEEN MOMENTS

"Abigail, his wife, was discerning and beautiful, but Nabal was harsh and badly behaved." (1 Samuel 25:3)

Have you ever wondered if your quiet faithfulness matters? If all those small decisions you make when no-one is watching are actually preparing you for something bigger?

Abigail was a discerning and beautiful woman whose quiet faith and courage contrasted sharply to her very rich but "harsh and badly behaved" husband, Nabal.

David—already anointed as future king but hiding in the wilderness—had been protecting Nabal's flocks. When he asked for provisions and Nabal insulted him, David vowed to destroy the entire household. It was Abigail's intervention that changed everything.

When we first meet Abigail, she seems to appear out of nowhere. But there's something remarkable about how quickly she springs into action when crisis strikes.

Maybe, behind the scenes, Abigail had been quietly using her wisdom—pursuing God, handling the weight of living with such a foolish man.

All those quiet things that no-one sees—in the quiet of your own heart, in the quiet of your own home—are not wasted. And in this moment, they become deeply relevant.

Maybe you're in a season right now where you feel unseen or unimportant. You're faithfully showing up, day after day, dealing with challenges that nobody else sees or understands.

Perhaps you're having to deal with someone difficult in your life. Someone foolish, or proud, or reckless.

But here's what Abigail's story reminds us: Every time you've whispered, "God, give me wisdom for this"—your faithfulness in the small things, your decision to trust God even when you can't see the bigger picture—none of it is wasted. It's shaping you for a purpose that may not be clear to you yet, but God sees it.

All those quiet, faithful decisions—the times you've leaned in to hear His voice—the unseen moments that nobody notices—they matter.

God sees every one.

Reflection:

Your quiet moments of faithfulness are never wasted. God sees every one.

Prayer:

Lord, help me to be faithful in the quiet moments. When I can't see the bigger picture, help me trust that You are using even the ordinary days to shape me for Your purposes. Amen.

FORTY-FOUR
COURAGE TO DO WHAT'S RIGHT

"Then Abigail quickly took bread, wine, and provisions, and loaded them on donkeys." (1 Samuel 25:18 paraphrased)

Have you ever had to act first and ask permission later?

Abigail did. And the stakes couldn't have been higher.

David had sent his young men to Nabal's house on a feast day and reminded him how they had cared for his flock. He'd asked Nabal to treat his young men with favour, fully expecting him to welcome them as honoured guests.

David's request was humble and respectful, but instead of responding with gratitude, Nabal mocked him: 'Who is this David?'

But this wasn't just anybody that Nabal was dissing and dismissing—it was the future King. Major mistake!

So David told his 400 men to strap on their swords to avenge this insult! David wasn't just coming for Nabal—he intended to wipe out every male in his household. Abigail's life was at stake too.

One of Nabal's servants went to Abigail and told her what had happened. This was Abigail's moment.

She commanded her servants to bake bread, to take wine, grain, figs, and raisins, then she jumped on a donkey and went out to face David and his 400 bloodthirsty men. She was no ordinary woman!

It's interesting that she said to her servants, "take all these things," but told them, "don't tell my husband." This isn't about ignoring wise counsel—Nabal wasn't offering wisdom. He was being foolish. And his foolishness was about to cost lives.

But maybe there's someone in your life who has authority but lacks wisdom. Not someone offering godly counsel you'd rather not hear—but someone whose fear, foolishness, or need for control, is blocking what God is clearly calling you to do.

I'm not suggesting you be deceitful or undermine legitimate authority. But there are times when we must act on the wisdom God has given us, even when those around us cannot see it.

Sometimes, we just need to do the thing we feel led by God to do. And ask permission afterwards.

This is exactly what Abigail did.

That quiet conviction isn't foolishness. Often, it's God-given wisdom. And sometimes courage means trusting it.

Reflection:

Sometimes God calls you to act with courage, even when others can't see the wisdom in what you're doing.

Prayer: *Lord, give me the courage to act on the wisdom You give me. Amen.*

FORTY-FIVE
THE POWER OF HUMILITY

"On me alone, my lord, be the guilt. Please let your servant speak in your ears and hear the words of your servant." (1 Samuel 25:24)

Have you ever felt powerless to change a situation you were stuck in?

Abigail could so easily have seen herself as powerless, but she didn't. She realised she had a choice—and responded with great courage and wisdom.

She rode out to meet David—not on a fine horse, but on a donkey, signalling humility and peace. When she reached him, she jumped down, fell face down, and bowed low before him.

And then she spoke. "On me alone, my Lord, be the guilt. Please let your servant speak in your ears and hear the words of your servant."

She accepted the blame for the foolishness of her husband, and begged him to "forgive the trespasses of your maidservant," taking on her shoulders the sins of her husband.

With these simple words she turned the mess her husband had created into an opportunity for peace.

There's an echo of Jesus here. He would ride a donkey into Jerusalem, showing He came in peace. And He would take on sins that weren't His—absorbing the consequences so relationship could be restored.

Abigail did both.

How different this is from our natural response when someone close to us makes a mistake! Our instinct can often be to protect ourselves, to deny any involvement and to distance ourselves from potential fallout.

But Abigail shows us a different way.

Maybe you're in a situation right now where you don't have the power to change anything. But like Abigail, you can choose how you respond.

She couldn't control Nabal. She couldn't control David's rage. But she could control how she responded.

That's where her power lay. Not in changing her circumstances—but in choosing wisdom, humility, and courage in the midst of them.

Reflection:

You're never as powerless as you feel. You can always choose how you respond.

Prayer:

Lord, when I feel stuck and powerless, remind me that I always have a choice—how I respond, how I show up, how I trust You. Amen.

FORTY-SIX
SPEAKING TRUTH WITH WISDOM

"When the Lord has done all he promised and has made you leader of Israel, don't let this be a blemish on your record." (1 Samuel 25:30)

When you need someone to hear hard truth, how do you get through to them?

In her encounter with David, Abigail didn't plead for her own life or her husband's. She did something far wiser.

She showed David why it would be bad for *him* to take revenge. She focused on the effect on *him* as a future leader and as a man of God.

That's true wisdom.

So often we argue from the point of view of how things will affect us. Abigail argued from how it would affect him.

She seemed to know what God had promised David: "When the Lord has done all he promised and has made you leader of Israel, don't let this be a blemish on your record."

And she wasn't afraid to speak the truth, with great respect. She spoke the hard truth to David, but couched it in wise and gentle words.

She reminded David that God is the One who avenges, and that it's not for man to avenge himself, when she said "As the Lord lives, and as your soul lives, because the Lord has restrained you from bloodguilt and from saving with your own hand…"

Speaking hard truth is never easy, especially when emotions are running high. But Abigail shows us that when we speak with wisdom, respect, and genuine concern for others' best interests, even difficult truths can be heard.

She focused on what David needed to hear—not her own years of pain and frustration with Nabal, not her own fear of what might happen next.

So next time you need someone to understand you, or you need to speak hard truth, try framing it from their viewpoint.

Argue from *their* perspective, not yours. What do *they* need to hear? What's at stake for *them*?

That's true wisdom.

Reflection:

Your voice, grounded in God's wisdom and genuine concern for others, can change the course of someone's story.

Prayer:

Lord, help me see beyond my own perspective to what's truly best for others. Give me courage to speak Your truth with love. Amen.

FORTY-SEVEN
THE COURAGE TO BE CORRECTED

"Blessed is the Lord God of Israel, who sent you this day to meet me! And blessed is your advice and blessed are you, because you have kept me this day from coming to bloodguilt and from avenging myself with my own hand." (1 Samuel 25:32-33)

When was the last time you admitted you were wrong? Have you ever had to do it in front of other people?

Just imagine the scene. David says, "Come on guys, strap on your swords," and his men are ready for a fight, their bloodlust is up. And then he has to backtrack—to acknowledge that he's about to make a huge mistake.

With his 400 fighting men looking on, he acknowledges Abigail's wisdom, saying, 'You have kept me this day from coming to bloodshed and from avenging myself with my own hand.'

Think about that. David is their leader, yet he publicly backtracks in front of 400 men. That takes a different kind of courage.

His next impulse was to thank God, as he realised that his desire for revenge had nearly led him to commit bloodshed. He encouraged Abigail to return home, promising her that he would not kill her husband.

David could've wrecked his future with one rash act. Yet he readily admitted his mistake—saw God's hand in the words of this stranger whose husband had offended him.

True leaders are humble. They can admit when they're wrong.

Jesus—the greatest leader who ever lived—was the humblest of them all. And David, the man after God's own heart, showed that same quality here.

As we mature in life and faith, you'd think we'd get better at receiving correction. Yet often the opposite proves true. Pride can grow alongside our experience, making it increasingly difficult to admit when we're in the wrong.

Maybe you've been the one others look to for wisdom. And somewhere along the way, it's become harder to say "I got that wrong." It feels embarrassing. Like you should know better by now.

But humility isn't about thinking less of yourself. It's about thinking of yourself less—and being willing to hear what God might be saying through others.

Reflection:

True leadership isn't about never making mistakes—it's being humble enough to admit when you have.

Prayer:

Lord, give me the humility to receive correction gracefully. Make me teachable, like David. Like Jesus. Amen.

FORTY-EIGHT
LET GOD HANDLE IT!

"Blessed be the Lord, who has pleaded the cause of my reproach from the hand of Nabal, and has kept His servant from evil!" (1 Samuel 25:39)

Have you ever caught yourself thinking, "That's so unfair"? When someone wrongs us—whether it's the car that just cut us up, or the person who hurt you deeply and never even said sorry—something in us wants to see them face the consequences.

When Abigail returned home, she found her husband Nabal having a wild and drunken party. Wisely she said nothing.

It wasn't till the morning that she told him what had happened. When he realised how his insult had nearly cost them all their lives, he had a stroke and died a few days later.

Nabal paid the ultimate price for his disrespect to David. God's judgment on Nabal was a form of divine justice—not just for David, but also for Abigail.

God saved David from two kinds of evil—not just bloodguilt, but from taking matters into his own hands. He stepped back. God stepped in.

For Abigail, who had lived many years with this foolish man, it seems likely she had suffered deeply. But now, she too was vindicated.

This is one of the hardest lessons to learn. When someone treats us badly—especially when we've been kind to them—our natural instinct is to want immediate justice. We want them to understand how they've hurt us. We want them to face consequences.

We want revenge.

It's not having these thoughts that's wrong, but what we choose to do with them.

Deuteronomy 32:35 reminds us, *"Vengeance is mine, I will repay, says the Lord."*

This story challenges us to give our pain to God, trust His timing, and believe that His justice will prevail.

David stepped back. God stepped in.

What if we did the same?

Reflection:

God sees every injustice you've endured and every tear you've shed. His justice may be delayed, but it is never denied.

Prayer:

Lord, help me to trust You with the injustices in my life. When I'm tempted to take revenge, remind me that vengeance belongs to You. Give me the patience to wait for Your timing. Amen.

FORTY-NINE
WHEN IT'S TIME FOR A NEW CHAPTER

"So David received from her hand what she had brought him, and said to her, 'Go up in peace to your house.'" (1 Samuel 25:35)

The woman who had endured years with a foolish husband now became wife to David—the warrior king with the heart of a shepherd boy.

Soon afterwards, David sent for her and made her his wife, and she became part of his household.

Her story ends well because of her wisdom, gentle nature, humility, and trust in God. Those same qualities are what He still treasures in us today.

She is a real example of what it says in 1 Peter 3, verses 3 to 4: *'let your adorning be the hidden person of the heart with the imperishable beauty of a gentle and quiet spirit, which in God's sight is very precious.'*

Abigail didn't just stumble into this moment.

She had been growing these qualities through all those hard years with Nabal. When her moment came, she was ready.

She chose to lead herself. She didn't wait for someone else to lead her, to guide her, or to show her the way—she sought God, she listened for His voice, and she let Him shape her character. She took responsibility for her own spiritual growth.

And, after years of waiting, her moment came—and she stepped up and into it with courage and wisdom.

And God turned her situation around.

She went from being wife to a foolish, arrogant man, to being wife of a man after God's own heart.

Her story shows us something powerful. As she walked faithfully with the wisdom and gifts God had given her, He opened the door to her next step. She didn't force it. She grew—and then God moved.

If you're in a season of waiting right now, however you got here, whatever's happening, don't waste it.

Seek God. Listen for His voice. Ask Him to shape you—so when your moment comes, you're ready.

After years of waiting, God turned Abigail's situation around, and He can do the same for you.

Reflection:

God is often doing His deepest work in you when circumstances feel most challenging.

Prayer:

Lord, use this season to shape me. Grow in me a gentle and quiet spirit that is precious in Your sight. Amen.

PART 8

WHEN THE WORLD SAYS YOU'RE DONE—BUT GOD SAYS THERE'S MORE

FIFTY
THE STRENGTH OF QUIET DEFIANCE

"But the midwives feared God and did not do as the king of Egypt commanded them, but let the boys live." (Exodus 1:17)

Have you ever found yourself in a situation where doing the right thing felt impossible? When the rules say one thing, but to comply goes against your conscience?

That's where we meet two hidden heroes—Shiphrah and Puah.

A new Pharaoh had risen to power who oppressed the Israelites cruelly. And yet, the more the people were oppressed, the more they thrived. This struck fear into Pharaoh's heart. In desperation, he decided to kill every Hebrew baby boy at birth.

So, he summoned Shiphrah and Puah—two Hebrew midwives—and commanded them to carry out his order.

Can you imagine standing before the most powerful man in the land, being told to commit murder—knowing that to refuse could cost you your life?

These were ordinary women. They spent their days bringing life into the world—and now they were being asked to take it.

All these women knew was four hundred years of slavery and oppression. They had no idea their quiet act of defiance was part of God's plan to deliver an entire nation through Moses.

They refused Pharaoh's order. Why? The Bible tells us simply: the midwives feared God—they trusted Him more than they feared Pharaoh.

When he demanded an explanation, they gave him a partial truth—that the Hebrew women gave birth too quickly. Behind their careful words was a bold decision to obey God rather than man.

Notice this detail: Pharaoh is not named. Yet the Bible records the names of Shiphrah and Puah—two ordinary women, remembered forever.

Maybe you're facing a similar choice—do the right thing, or follow the crowd?

The midwives' fear of God gave them courage to defy the most powerful man on earth.

When we choose to fear God more than man—when we choose His approval over human approval—our quiet acts of obedience can have far greater impact than we ever imagined.

Reflection:

Sometimes the most powerful act of faith is the quiet refusal to follow the crowd.

Prayer:

Lord, when it's hard to do the right thing, give me courage. Give me strength to choose Your way over what will please others. Amen.

FIFTY-ONE
SMALL ACTS WITH GREAT IMPACT

"Therefore God dealt well with the midwives; and the people multiplied and grew very mighty." (Exodus 1:20)

Have you ever wondered if your small, quiet choices really make a difference?

Shiphrah and Puah couldn't have known what their act of defiance would set in motion. But their refusal to obey Pharaoh was about much more than saving babies—it was the first step in setting God's people free.

For four hundred years, the people of Israel had known only obedience to their oppressors. The midwives faithfulness and quiet obedience was about to break the chains of four centuries of slavery.

Pharaoh expected them to spread his murderous command to every Hebrew birth. Instead, they defied him. What courage it must have taken to stand firm in such a moment!

They couldn't see the whole plan, but they were faithful to their conscience. They trusted that God would honour their faithfulness.

And He did.

Pharaoh set out to destroy a nation, but God used two women to begin setting His people free.

And God blessed them. God gave them children and households—a profound reward in their culture.

Maybe you feel like what you do each day doesn't really matter. A kind word here, a quiet prayer there—who notices?

God does.

Your quiet faith, your hidden courage—these are never unseen by Him. Even the smallest act of faithfulness can ripple outward, in ways we may never see.

God can use even the quietest acts of courage to shape history. He wrote Shiphrah and Puah's names into His story. He can do the same with yours.

Reflection:

You don't need to see how it all fits together—you just need to say 'yes' to God, and trust Him with the rest.

Prayer:

Father, help me to obey You even when I can't see the whole plan. Give me courage to be faithful in the small things, trusting that You will use each one to write Your story. Amen.

FIFTY-TWO
WHEN TRUSTING GOD TAKES COURAGE

"By faith Moses' parents hid him for three months after he was born, because they saw he was no ordinary child, and they were not afraid of the king's edict." (Hebrews 11:23)

How do you feel when the future is uncertain and you can't control the outcome?

After the midwives' refusal to obey Pharaoh, his rage increased. He issued a new decree—this time to all his people: every Hebrew boy must be thrown into the Nile, but the girls could live. It was a command meant to destroy a generation and wipe out the future of God's people.

And it's here that we meet Jochebed, Moses's mother.

She and her husband, Amram, were both from the tribe of Levi—the tribe set apart for spiritual leadership, priestly service, and carrying out God's purposes. Their family was destined to be part of God's plan in a profound way, though they could not yet see how.

When Jochebed gave birth to a son, Scripture tells us he was a *fine child.* Now, this wasn't just a way of saying, "What a beautiful baby." Every mother thinks that! The Hebrew word here is the same used when God declared His creation "good."

There was something different, something set apart about this child. Acts 7:20 calls him "no ordinary child," and Hebrews 11:23 tells us his parents hid him, "not being afraid of the king's edict." So Jochebed hid him for three months.

Can you imagine the courage that took? Every cry, every knock at the door, every whisper in the street must have struck fear into her heart.

Yet she kept trusting. Day after day, she did what she could—nursing, rocking, silencing his cries—while leaving the outcome in God's hands. She didn't try to control every detail of the future.

That's what trusting God's timing looks like: doing your part faithfully, then releasing what you cannot control.

Maybe you're in a similar place. Perhaps you're facing a season where the future looks different than you imagined or feels uncertain. Like Jochebed, you're being asked to trust God with the outcome.

Sometimes faith simply asks us to do our part day by day, and let God carry those things that are too heavy for us.

Reflection:

Trusting God doesn't mean having it all figured out—it means taking the next step, even when you can't see where it leads.

Prayer:

Lord, when the future feels uncertain, help me to trust You. Give me the courage for today, and help me let go of what I cannot control. Amen.

FIFTY-THREE
WHEN FAITH REQUIRES BOLD ACTION

"But when she could hide him no longer, she got a papyrus basket for him and coated it with tar and pitch. Then she placed the child in it and put it among the reeds along the bank of the Nile." (Exodus 2:3)

Have you ever felt torn between two impossible choices?

When Moses could no longer be hidden—when his cries grew louder, when the risk of discovery became too great—Jochebed faced an agonising decision.

But what could she do? She could not protect him or silence him forever.

So she prepared a papyrus basket, waterproofed it carefully with tar and pitch—because his very life depended on it—and placed him inside. Then, with trembling hands, she set the basket among the reeds of the Nile.

On the surface, it looked like she was obeying Pharaoh's decree. After all, hadn't she cast her son into the Nile, just as he had commanded?

But in reality, she was acting in faith—with incredible courage. Placing her firstborn baby son in a basket on the river may have looked like surrender to Pharaoh, but she was actually surrendering to God—trusting Him for the outcome, when things looked bleak and impossible.

Then, it *"just so happened"* that Pharaoh's daughter came to bathe at the river. What seemed like coincidence was actually divine orchestration.

She saw the basket, sent her servant to fetch it, and when she opened it, the baby cried.

Scripture says she "felt sorry for him," but the Hebrew meaning goes deeper. The word expresses compassion in the face of power—the choice to spare when you could destroy. Pharaoh's daughter had the authority to end his life. Instead, she chose to save him.

Maybe God is asking you to place something precious into His hands? Maybe you've done all you can and now you must release the outcome to Him?

Jochebed's situation must have felt impossible. She could keep hiding him—but for how long? Or she could obey Pharaoh's decree and lose him forever.

Two impossible choices. Until God showed her a third.

Do what you can. Then trust Him with the rest.

Reflection:

Faith isn't choosing between holding on or giving up—it's doing what you can and trusting God with what you can't.

Prayer:

Father, help me trust You to hold what I cannot control. Amen.

FIFTY-FOUR
WHAT HAPPENS WHEN YOU LET GO …

"By faith Moses, when he had grown up, refused to be known as the son of Pharaoh's daughter. He chose to be mistreated along with the people of God rather than to enjoy the fleeting pleasures of sin." (Hebrews 11:24–25)

Have you ever had to let go—of something, or someone—and trust that God would take it from there?

As Pharaoh's daughter discovered the baby and drew him from the river, Miriam seized the moment. She approached the princess and offered to find a Hebrew woman to nurse the child—and Jochebed was called back to nurse her son.

Imagine her joy! The baby boy she had released into the Nile was placed back in her arms. And she was now being paid to do the very thing her heart longed for: to love, nurture, and raise him.

So Jochebed took Moses home. For three to five years, until he was weaned, she nursed him, held him, and whispered the truths of God into his heart. Those early years she had with him mattered more than she could have known.

Jochebed used her time well. She taught him who he was, planted seeds of faith, seeds that would later bear fruit when he grew into the man God had called him to be.

When Moses was returned to Pharaoh's daughter, he was given an Egyptian name and raised in the palace as her adopted son.

As a prince, he received the finest education. Yet what he learned from his mother never left him. The seeds she planted remained deep inside him.

Years later, when God called Moses back to stand before Pharaoh and demand the freedom of God's people, we see the fruit of the seeds Jochebed planted in his early days.

Moses was raised in the very house of the one who wanted to destroy him. Pharaoh, the one oppressing God's people, educated and trained the very man that God would use to free His people. God was preparing the deliverer right under the enemy's nose.

Maybe you're in a season of letting go—of children, roles, or dreams. It can feel like your influence is ending.

But here's what Jochebed's story shows us: her greatest impact happened after she released her child into God's hands.

When you let go, God steps in.

Reflection:

Letting go isn't the end of your influence—it's where God steps in.

Prayer:

Lord, help me to hand over to You the things I cannot control, and trust You to take it from here. Amen.

FIFTY-FIVE
WHEN YOUR QUIET LOVE MATTERS

"There was a believer in Joppa named Tabitha (which in Greek is Dorcas). She was always doing kind things for others and helping the poor. About that time she became sick and died, and her body was washed and placed in an upstairs room." (Acts 9:36-37)

Have you ever wondered if the small kindnesses you show really make a difference?

Tabitha's story takes place in the coastal town of Joppa. The Bible describes her as a disciple—the only woman actually given that title.

To be called a disciple meant she was known as a follower of Jesus, someone who tried to live as He did. The book of Acts tells us, "She spent her life doing kind things for others and serving the poor."

Tabitha worked with her hands, creating garments for the widows in her community. She gave these women dignity—they became part of a community of valued and loved women, this love signified by the garments she handmade for them.

Each stitch she sewed was a quiet expression of love, love folded into every seam, each garment a declaration of their worth.

In that culture, widows were outcasts, often dependent on charity to survive. Yet Tabitha's love and acts of kindness restored their dignity, their worth, their humanity.

Tabitha didn't focus on what she didn't have, she simply did what she could with what she had. She used her skill with needle and thread—to love well, to help these women see their value, and to invite them into community.

Maybe you've wondered if your gifts are too ordinary to matter? Maybe you've compared yourself to others, and felt that what you have to offer is too small to make a difference? Or that your gifts have to be acknowledged by others to really count?

Tabitha's story shows us that we don't have to wait for anyone, we don't even have to have much in our hands, we just have to use the small gifts we've been given, and share them with others.

Your quiet acts of service matter—the meals you've prepared, the listening ears you've offered, the love you show in ordinary moments, the small kindnesses you've shown. Each of these matters, because, in God's hands, they can make a difference.

You may never see the impact this side of heaven, but God does.

Reflection:

You don't need any special gifts to be someone who changes lives—you just need to show love.

Prayer:

Father, help me to love well today. Use whatever gifts You've given me, however small they might seem, to help others see their worth in Your eyes. Amen.

FIFTY-SIX
WHEN LOVE BECOMES YOUR LEGACY

"When Peter arrived, he was greeted by the sight of many widows weeping—many of them showing him the tunics and other garments that Tabitha had made." (Acts 9:39)

Think of the people who've made a really significant and positive impact on your life—how many were because of their skills, and how many were because of their kindness or their love?

Can you imagine the scene? These women crowded around Peter, showing how Tabitha had loved them.

With each stitch, each quiet prayer, she had changed how they saw themselves. Every garment she sewed declared their value. She helped them see what God had always seen—that they were worthy of love.

But when she died, that new identity was threatened. The women who had been seen, valued, loved—once again faced becoming poor, unseen widows, dependent on handouts. They wept not only for her loss, but for the loss of who they'd become through her love.

Perhaps you've felt invisible at times—overlooked or ignored?

Tabitha understood that feeling. But instead of letting it define her, her ability to see others became her gift.

She saw the ones holding back, the ones feeling left out or lonely. She responded by helping them feel seen and valued.

Because when you've felt invisible, you know how to see others. You can become the one who notices—and reminds them of their worth.

And that's what really matters.

You don't need a title or a platform to change lives. You don't need anyone's permission. You just need love.

Because only love has the power to restore dignity. Only love can help others see their God-given worth. Only love has the power to bring life to those who feel they're beyond hope.

When we stand before God, it won't be our achievements that matter most.

So, instead of worrying about your place in life, in church, or in your family, there's only one question you need to ask yourself.

Have you loved well?

Not perfectly. Not flawlessly. But well.

The love you show today—those simple, quiet acts of kindness—has the power to change the world.

Reflection:

You may never know whose life you've changed by simply choosing to love well.

Prayer:

Father, today, please help me to love well. Amen.

CONCLUSION - THE GOD WHO STILL SEES

As a woman, you know what it is to feel unseen.

We've walked with women who've shown us courage, faith, perseverance and love—the very qualities you need to face your world today.

Many of them were unseen for most of their lives, yet each was known, valued and called by God.

For some, being seen by Him didn't immediately change their circumstances. But it changed everything about how they faced them.

And as they walked with Him, His hand was at work — moulding, shaping, and ultimately bringing fruit from even the hardest seasons.

Even in their darkest moments, God saw them — and met them there, in the middle of it all. That's who He is. That's who He's always been.

He sees you too.

Whatever season you're in — whether you're stepping out in faith or simply putting one foot in front of the other — hear this:

You are not invisible.

God sees you. He notices. He cares.

He is writing your story and His story, weaving them together.

You are seen. You are known. And you are deeply, deeply loved.

Prayer:

Father, thank You that I am seen, known and loved — not for what I do, but for who I am. Thank You that You see me — really see me. Help me rest in that today. Amen.

ONE MORE THING

Thank you for being here. For taking time to let these women's stories speak to your heart. As an independent author, it means more than you know.

If something in these pages has touched you, I'd be so grateful if you'd share a quick review on Amazon.

It's one of the best ways to help other women discover this book — and I'd love to hear what you thought.

AN INVITATION

Before you close this book, there's one more story I want to share with you.

There's something that most people miss about Martha's story.

Bethany, where Martha lived, was only a couple of miles from Jerusalem. When Jesus told His disciples, "Let's go to Bethany," their response was, "Do you really want to go back there? Last time they tried to stone You!"

And yet—for the sake of His friends—Jesus still went. He knew it would anger the religious leaders. He knew it would lead to His death. And it did.

After He raised Lazarus, some rushed back to Jerusalem and told the Pharisees. From that point on, the religious leaders were committed to killing Jesus.

The miracle that saved Martha's brother sealed Jesus's fate.

He knew what it would cost Him. And He came anyway.

For Martha. For Mary. For Lazarus.

And for you. Right where you are.

That's the kind of love Jesus offers. Costly, personal, and yours.

As you've walked with these invisible women, perhaps you've felt drawn to know Him for yourself. Maybe you're wondering how you can experience the same transforming love these women found.

Just as Jesus met each of these women exactly where they were, He wants to meet you today. Here's what the Bible says:

> *"God loved the world so much that he gave his only Son, so that everyone who believes in him will have eternal life and never be lost."*
>
> JOHN 3:16 MSG

If you'd like to begin your own relationship with Jesus, you can talk to Him right now.

Here's a simple prayer to help you:

Lord Jesus,

Thank you for loving me just as I am. I am sorry for living life my own way. Thank you that you died for me, rose from the dead, and are alive today. Please forgive me and make me new.

I invite you into my life—fill me with your Holy Spirit. I choose to follow you today and always.

Amen.

If you just prayed that prayer — welcome! Heaven is celebrating. Your new life with Jesus has begun.

Like the women in these stories, you too can experience His healing, freedom, and purpose.

His Holy Spirit now lives in you, giving you everything you need for the journey ahead.

Here are some simple next steps:

—Tell another Christian about your decision to follow Jesus

—Start reading your Bible—get a Bible or download a Bible app

—Find a church where you can be encouraged and supported

—Talk to Jesus each day—just as these women did

Just like each woman in this book, God has good plans for you.

Your story with Him is just beginning.

ABOUT THE AUTHOR

Jennifer knows what it feels like to be invisible.

After divorce, seasons of doubt, and years of wondering if she had anything to offer, she discovered that God had never stopped seeing her — and He wasn't finished writing her story yet.

Today, her passion is helping Christian women step fully into the purpose God has for them. She has three grown-up children and eleven grandchildren. She enjoys time at her beachside apartment in the south of England and her small cottage in rural Sweden.

You may enjoy some of her other books, including:

Women of Courage — explore thirty-one Bible women whose stories are often overlooked.

They weren't perfect—but through faith, they stepped into God's purposes and did extraordinary things.

Learning to Live in Challenging Times — through the timeless biblical story of Ruth, Naomi, and Boaz, discover encouragement for navigating life's challenges.

Their story offers assurance that your life matters and guidance for finding hope and purpose, even in unexpected circumstances.

Daily Readings for Difficult Days — Jennifer wrote these simple, encouraging readings to help women through difficult seasons, following her own struggle with divorce and raising three teenagers as a single mom.

You can find all Jennifer's books and audiobooks (including translations) on Amazon and other popular platforms.

SAMPLE CHAPTER FROM WOMEN OF COURAGE

As Jesus was on his way, the crowds almost crushed him. And a woman was there who had been subject to bleeding for twelve years, but no-one could heal her. She came up behind him and touched the edge of his cloak, and immediately her bleeding stopped.

"Who touched me?" Jesus asked. When they all denied it, Peter said, "Master, the people are crowding and pressing against you."

But Jesus said, "Someone touched me; I know that power has gone out from me."

Then the woman, seeing that she could not go unnoticed, came trembling and fell at his feet. In the presence of all the people, she told why she had touched him and how she had been instantly healed. Then he said to her, "Daughter, your faith has healed you. Go in peace."

Luke 8:42-48

How many times should we pray for healing before quitting? Once? Twice? Ten times? A hundred? After repeatedly asking for prayer, wouldn't you begin to feel a little self-conscious or embarrassed? Perhaps twinges of discouragement or cynicism would creep into your heart, causing you to doubt God's promises and wonder whether He truly cares for you.

Most of us have something in our lives that we're ashamed of, something we want to hide, something we're thankful our church friends don't know.

But what if that hidden shame was public knowledge, laid bare for all your neighbours and friends to see? What if you couldn't hide your shameful thoughts or actions anymore?

This is how this woman must have felt. For years, she sought healing in vain. She had spent all of her money on doctors who couldn't help.

In Jewish culture, she was considered unclean; her neighbours saw her constant bleeding as a shameful condition. Through the years, friends and family probably ostracised her, leaving her feeling isolated. People likely whispered that some secret sin must be causing her suffering.

Yet she hadn't given up hope. She still had just enough faith, (though it may have been as small as a mustard seed), to push through the crowd that surrounded Jesus. In her condition, she shouldn't have been amidst the crowd at all, but she defied convention to come to Jesus.

She didn't dare try to get His attention, lest she draw attention to her shameful self. And what if He, too, turned her away? She couldn't bear to be rejected again, yet she knew deep down that Jesus was someone special—that somehow, just by getting close to Him, her life could be changed. And so, in an act of desperation, she reached out and touched the edge of His cloak as He passed by.

His power healed her immediately. But even when she took His power without His permission, Jesus didn't turn from her as everyone else had.

In His words, "Daughter, your faith has healed you, go in peace," He told her the three things that she had so longed to hear: She was accepted as a daughter, she was healed and she would finally experience peace.

After years of living in shame, she finally experienced acceptance. For the first time since she was a girl, she was free to live a normal life. Finally, she knew the peace that she had sought for so many years.

Jesus is the same yesterday, today, and forever. He desires to restore you from years of pain, shame, and discouragement. He wants to heal the places where you ache physically and emotionally.

Reflection Questions

Is there something that you're remembering, even now, that makes you feel ashamed or that you want to hide from others?

....

....

....

Jesus didn't turn away from the woman when she touched Him. Instead, He affirmed her faith and restored her dignity. How does this demonstrate Jesus' heart for you when you're hurting and ashamed?

....

....

....

You are "precious in the sight of the Lord" (Isaiah 43:4). Are you ready to let Jesus restore your sense of worth? What steps can you take to embrace your identity as God's precious child?

....

....

....

What might it look like to bring your pain and shame to Jesus and ask Him to touch and change your life?

....

....

....

SAMPLE CHAPTER FROM LEARNING TO LIVE IN CHALLENGING TIMES

Now it came about in the days when the judges governed, that there was a famine in the land. And a man of Bethlehem in Judah went to reside in the land of Moab with his wife and his two sons. The name of the man was Elimelech, and the name of his wife, Naomi; and the names of his two sons were Mahlon and Chilion, Ephrathites of Bethlehem in Judah. So they entered the land of Moab and remained there.

Then Elimelech, Naomi's husband, died; and she was left with her two sons. And they took for themselves Moabite women as wives; the name of the one was Orpah, and the name of the other, Ruth. And they lived there about ten years. Then both Mahlon and Chilion also died, and the woman was left without her two sons and her husband.

Ruth 1:1-5 (NASB)

As famine crept into every home and heart, a shadow fell across the land of Judah. Elimelech stood at the threshold of his home. The famine's grip seemed to tighten with each passing day, crushing his dreams of a prosperous future for his family.

Elimelech's wife, Naomi, stood by his side. Together, they had weathered many storms, but this famine threatened to consume all they had worked so hard for. Elimelech had a difficult decision to make: stay in Bethlehem and trust God to provide, or seek sustenance far from home, in the land of Moab.

Elimelech chose to leave his homeland, hoping to find safety and security for his family. Little did he know that this decision, born of desperation and fear, would set in motion a series of events that would forever change the course of their lives.

Life often presents us with crossroads where important decisions must be made. We've all faced moments of uncertainty where our faith is tested and the way forward seems unclear.

In these times, it can be all too easy to rely on our own understanding, to leave God out of the equation and allow fear to guide our choices.

But as we see from Elimelech's story, our decisions have far-reaching consequences, not just for ourselves, but for those we love. Though he sought to escape trouble, Elimelech's choice to leave Bethlehem and settle in Moab ended in tragedy, leaving his wife Naomi and daughters-in-law as widows, facing poverty and hardship.

Making such choices can feel overwhelming. We can fear making the wrong choice, or wonder which path to take. These are the questions that Elimelech also faced.

Because we know how his story ends, it can be easy for us to judge Elimelech's decision, but the truth is, we've all had moments where we've struggled to discern God's will or faced choices where we've allowed our fears to overshadow our faith.

Making the right decision can be far harder than it seems. Sometimes the road branches in two and our choice is not always clear. Perhaps we push on a door that seems to shut in our face, but struggle to know whether God is saying no or if we should press on in faith? Or perhaps we become impatient, trying to rush God into speaking, when His plan is for us to grow and learn during the waiting?

It's at times like these, when we face hard decisions, that it's helpful to remember that God wants to guide us. Just as He led men and women in the pages of our Bibles, He promises to show us the way today.

When faced with life's challenges, will we stop, wait, and look for the clues to see what God is saying? What if, instead of leaning on our own understanding, we took the time to seek God's guidance?

Our Father promises to lead and guide us when we seek Him. He promises to always show us where to go, as expressed in Isaiah 58:11 (MSG): "*I will always show you where to go. I'll give you a full life in the emptiest of places.*"

As we will see, God left Elimelech plenty of clues, but he chose to ignore them all:

- Elimelech's name means "*God is King.*" However, when it was Elimelech's turn to decide whether God would be the king of his life, his faith and courage wavered.

- Bethlehem, the town where he lived, means 'bread basket'. Why did he leave a place where its very name reminded him that God promised to provide?

- The people of Moab were descendants of Lot and his oldest daughter, who had an incestuous relationship (Genesis 19:37). Because of that, Moab was a place God wanted His people to avoid. Yet, Elimelech ignored this.

- God called the Israelites to remain pure and worship only Yahweh, the one true God (1 Kings 11:2; Exodus 20:3). Yet, the Moabites worshipped a false god named Chemosh.

- In Bethlehem, Elimelech and his family were surrounded by a supportive and loving community. When they moved away, they lost the wealth of close family relationships and friendships that God had given them.

- God's law stated that Israelites were not allowed to marry Moabite women, because they worshipped false gods. If they did, their descendants would be excluded from the assembly of the Lord for ten generations (Deuteronomy 23:3). Elimelech should have seen that there was no future for his sons in Moab.

- God had promised to provide for and sustain His people (Psalm 84:11 and Psalm 55:22). Elimelech forgot or ignored God's promises.

- Elimelech relied on his wealth to relocate his family. He uses his money as his solution rather than relying on God.

- Elimelech would have heard many stories of God rescuing His people from seemingly impossible situations. Yet he chose to ignore them, or think that the God who had rescued His people before, would not rescue them again. His decision was born from fear, not faith.

When my kids were young, I used to leave clues for them during Easter egg hunts. Each clue led to the next hiding place, and they would chase around the house to find the hidden treasures.

Similarly, God has hidden treasures of wisdom and guidance for us to discover. Just as the clues in an Easter egg hunt may not always be obvious, God's clues might not be immediately apparent either. However, they are there, waiting for us to seek them out.

He may speak or leave clues through what we read in our Bibles, through His promises, through friends, a Sunday sermon or even a billboard. He may speak to you in moments of silence, or through your dreams.

Or He may speak through your emotions and thoughts, a deep conviction or sense of which way you should turn, even though you don't quite understand why.

However, Elimelech allowed his fears to control his future. It would have required faith, courage, and strength of character for him to stay in Bethlehem, trust God, and wait for the famine to end. If we can learn from his mistakes, perhaps we can create a different future for ourselves and our families.

It can be tempting to think that one simple choice or a small step away from doing things God's way is insignificant. However, if we learn anything from Elimelech's story, it's that what we do can have a big impact on those we love the most.

Elimelech had no idea that his choice would have a wider impact than he could imagine, and most of the time, neither do we. Just as Elimelech's decision had far-reaching consequences, so too do our decisions. What we do has a ripple effect on the world around us. One wrong decision can have a significant impact, not only on our lives and the lives of those around us.

Whatever life choice or decision we are facing today, our Heavenly Father has left us clues as to the best way forward. Will we take the time to look for them? Will we wait, until we hear Him speak?

What ultimately shaped Elimelech's future was simple: his decision was rooted in fear. Being honest with ourselves about our feelings and fears, is our first step to learning to place our trust in God. Can we be honest enough to ask ourselves if our choices stem from fear rather than faith?

We all have fears, but it is what we do in the face of those fears that will define who we become. God encouraged Joshua to "*be strong and courageous*" three times in Joshua 1 alone.

Courage isn't the absence of fear; it's moving forward even when you're afraid.

Will we move forward in faith, trusting God, even when the outcomes seems uncertain? Hebrews 11:1 reminds us that "*faith is the assurance of things hoped for, the conviction of things not seen.*"

Your story isn't over just because you made one bad decision - or even if you've made dozens of bad choices. It takes courage to acknowledge that we've messed up. It can be hard to forgive ourselves, and even harder to ask God for forgiveness. Yet God is a God of forgiveness. Daniel 9:9 (NIV) tells us that God "*is merciful and forgiving, even though we have rebelled against him.*"

Romans 3:22 (NLT) tells us that "*We are made right with God by placing our faith in Jesus Christ.*" Once you've placed your faith and trust in Jesus, you're made right with God. You can be confident that every past sin is forgiven, your shame is covered, and your future in heaven is secure.

If you haven't yet put your trust in Jesus, you can find out more about this in the chapter 'Becoming A Christ Follower' at the end of this book.

Romans 8:28 says that "*in all things God works for the good of those who love him.*" This truth applies even when we make the wrong choice. God is sovereign. He can work through the wrong choices we've made in our lives.

As we'll see as we continue through Ruth's story, God can redeem even the darkest of situations, and He can redeem yours too.

We've seen how our decisions, whether rooted in fear or faith, can have far-reaching consequences for ourselves and those around us.

We've discovered that God is always speaking, leaving clues and treasures of wisdom for us to find when we take the time to seek Him.

As you continue your journey through this story, remember, God is at work, even through the difficult times. Be encouraged to trust in His guidance, for He is faithfully weaving purpose through every experience, even the ones we don't yet understand.

We all face choices that can shape our future. By seeking God's wisdom and following His clues, we can navigate life's challenges knowing that He is with us, even when the path ahead seems uncertain.

Time of Reflection

The story of Ruth and Naomi begins with a difficult decision that has far-reaching consequences.

What decisions or challenges are you facing today? What guidance do you sense God providing for your current situation?

....

....

....

Reflect on any 'clues' God might have already given you - perhaps through advice from a trusted friend, words that jump out as you read your Bible, a recurring thought, or a recent sermon.

....

....

....

Are there any Bible stories that speak to you about the decision or challenge you're currently facing? What Bible promises has God given you that can help you?

....

....

....

We often want an immediate answer, but sometimes we need to trust God's timing and wait. How might you ask for wisdom as you wait?

....

....

....

Elimelech relied on his wealth to solve his problems instead of trusting in God. In what areas of your life do you tend to rely on your own resources or abilities rather than trusting in God's provision?

....

....

....

Search your heart. What fears or past choices are weighing heavily on you? Name these fears and regrets below. Then, prayerfully consider how you can surrender these to God. How might you invite God to bring healing and restoration to these areas of your life?

....

....

....

Here's some words of hope:

Come now ... says the Lord: though your sins are like scarlet, they shall be as white as snow; though they are red like crimson, they shall become like wool.

Isaiah 1:18 (ESV)

Therefore, if anyone is in Christ, he is a new creation. The old has passed away; behold, the new has come.

2 Corinthians 5:17 (ESV)

www.ingramcontent.com/pod-product-compliance
Lightning Source LLC
Chambersburg PA
CBHW071206070526
44584CB00019B/2936